From Writing to Composing

An Introductory Composition Course

Beverly Ingram
Carol King

CAMBRIDGE
UNIVERSITY PRESS

Second Edition

CAMBRIDGE UNIVERSITY PRESS
Cambridge, New York, Melbourne, Madrid, Cape Town, Singapore, São Paulo, Delhi

Cambridge University Press
32 Avenue of the Americas, New York, NY 10013–2473, USA

www.cambridge.org
Information on this title: www.cambridge.org/9780521539142

First published 2004
4th printing 2008

Printed in the United States of America

A catalog record for this book is available from the British Library

Library of Congress Cataloging in Publication data
Ingram, Beverly, 1949–
From writing to composing: an introductory composition course / Beverly
Ingram, Carol King. – 2nd ed.
    p. cm.
ISBN 13: 978-0-521-53914-2
ISBN 10: 0-521-53914-5
1. English language – Textbooks for foreign speakers. 2. English language –
Composition and exercises. 3. Report writing. I. King, Carol, 1947– II. Title.
PE1128.I477 2004
808'.0428—dc22

Art direction and book design: Adventure House, NYC
Layout services: Page Designs International
Illustration credits: Dominic Bugatto/Three In a Box: pages 34, 35, 46, 56, 64, 67, 74, 82, 117;
    Jon Keegan: pages 26, 109, 110; Eric Larsen: page 38
Photography credits: page 15: ©Corbis; page 25: Clockwise from top left: ©Roy Morsch/Corbis;
    ©Leland Bobbe Studio/Corbis; ©Yellow Dog Productions/Getty Images; ©Ryan McVay/Getty Images;
    page 91: By permission from Merriam-Webster, Incorporated (www.Merriam-Webster.com); page 100:
    By permission from Seton Healthcare Network and Hixo, Inc.; page 111: ©Bettmann/Corbis

Table of Contents

PART TWO: Writing More, Writing Better

To the Teacher

What is *From Writing to Composing* all about?

From Writing to Composing, Second Edition, is a composition textbook for beginning and low-intermediate ESL/EFL students. While it retains the approach of the first edition – the interweaving of structured guided writing activities with freer composing activities that use a multi-draft approach – it has been radically transformed to reflect the evolution of writing instruction and the new technology available to student writers. New and updated tasks appear together with many of the original writing activities. All of the fourteen units are new.

What does the title *From Writing to Composing* mean?

The title refers to the way we approach teaching composition to lower-level students and the way that most units in the book are organized. Typical units develop a topic by moving students from guided *writing* activities to freer *composing* activities. Here are the basic differences between these two distinctly different types of activities:

1. A guided *writing* assignment is usually completed on the first try whereas a multi-draft *composition* is rarely, if ever, finished in one work session.

2. With guided *writing* activities, the teacher should expect students to pay close attention to both grammar and mechanics and will usually correct the assignments the first and probably only time that they are turned in. With *composing* activities, the teacher should generally ignore, and similarly encourage students to disregard, surface-level problems until the content has been revised at least once and is ready for editing.

3. A guided *writing* assignment is done primarily to practice English and is only for the teachers' scrutiny. *Composing,* on the other hand, has a purpose beyond learning the language and may have an audience other than the teacher.

4. A *writing* assignment probably does not deserve to be shown off in a class publication or on the classroom wall. A good *composition* does.

Writing activities and *composing* activities are equally important in a lower-level composition course. Lower-level students have relatively little language at their disposal, so they need a variety of guided writing activities that will give them something to say about a given topic and some language to say it with before confronting a composition assignment on the same topic. Then, after students have put their basic ideas down on paper, they need composing activities that will guide them through the process of rereading, rewriting, revising, and editing their work.

How is *From Writing to Composing* organized?

From Writing to Composing, Second Edition, has a two-part structure. Part One, *Getting Started,* introduces different genres of writing (such as letter writing, formal writing, and narrative) and the key activity types of the book.

Part Two, *Writing More, Writing Better,* teaches how to write paragraphs using different modes of rhetorical organization (such as enumeration, classification, and chronological order). The last unit teaches the basics of how to organize and write an essay.

Should I complete all units of the book?

Part One of the book is carefully designed to incorporate the components vital to a strong writing course for students at this level. Thus, every class should work with all of the units in this first part to establish the foundation for a well-rounded, effective course. In particular, teachers should work carefully through

Unit 4, *Sharing Stories*. This indispensable core unit introduces students, quite possibly for the first time in English, to the full multi-draft composing process.

Ideally, every class would also work through all of Part Two; however, given the dictates of time and curriculum as well as the needs of particular classes and students, it is often impossible to complete everything. Thus, Part Two gives teachers a body of material from which to choose according to the given situation.

From Part Two, in a shorter course, we recommend doing the four dictations in Units 7, 11, 12 and 14, two major "publishable" multi-draft compositions, and a portfolio containing less-polished compositions from other units. With lower-level students, we suggest doing the dictation sequences in Units 7, 11, 12, and 14, returning then to the freer composing activities in some of these units after students have developed more confidence through practice with other units. With higher-level students, we suggest doing more of the multi-draft compositions in Part Two and fewer of the structured composing activities.

Regardless of the circumstances, it is recommended that every student in every course complete and publish (or share) at least three multi-draft compositions. The first time students write a multi-draft composition, the purpose is to learn the composing process. The second time, they practice the process, and the third time, they establish some independence and confidence in using the process.

Should I finish one unit completely before beginning another?

Not necessarily. On any given day in the course, your students may be ready to start guided practice activities in one unit while still revising and editing a composition from a previous unit. This "overlap" makes for class sessions that have the variety needed to maintain student morale and interest.

Why are listening and speaking activities included?

Although the primary purpose of the book is to elicit a great deal of guided and free written work, a strong oral component is essential for lower-level students because they still need basic vocabulary on many common topics. Without oral work, many students would end up doing the guided activities intended to introduce key concepts and vocabulary by merely shuffling around on paper words they had never heard and could not pronounce. When it came time for the students to begin composing, these key words would still not be part of their active vocabulary, and they would be unable to handle the assignment.

Oral activities are also important because of the value lower-level students place on developing conversation skills and because such oral work helps some students overcome their fear of writing. As they talk through an activity, these students often gain confidence to face and eventually conquer their fear of pencil and paper or of writing on the computer.

How should I use computers?

As you use the book, you will sometimes see the computer icon (shown at left) in the margin beside both writing and composing activities. At this proficiency level, we recommend that students write and compose on the computer as much as possible so that they can revise and edit with ease. We also feel it is important for students to develop competence and speed in keyboarding, learn to take advantage of computer tools, such as the spell-check and word count, and use e-mail and the Internet comfortably. If available, a computer lab would be a good place to work on guided writing activities and timed independent writing.

How can I have my class do a newspaper or other publication? I know nothing about journalism or Web publishing.

Neither do we. Journalistic training is not necessary, and producing a professional product is not the point. The goal is to give students a reason to write well, a purpose for interacting, and a showcase for their finished work. Beginning with Unit 6, each unit suggests publication of the major composition of the unit via a class newspaper, magazine, or Web site or in a formal or informal wall or bulletin board display.

Although access to a computer is necessary for a class Web site, and a photocopy machine would be handy for the newspaper or magazine, your class can do the publication activities with little or no technology. The easiest method, for example, will often be a wall display that can be changed as the course progresses. "Unit 6 Class Publication," with its focus on a class newspaper or Web site, gives directions and examples to get started.

What are the main points about publications?

Whether your situation calls for newspaper, magazine, Web site, or wall, the central principles are the same.

1. Make an overall plan when you begin the course. Your school calendar, rather than the sequence of units in Part II, may be the best guide for scheduling your "publications." And, student computer know-how and school resources may guide your choice of format.

2. Vary the format of the publications if possible, so there are sometimes individual copies for students in the class to read and sometimes a single display copy in a public area or on a Web site for students in all classes to enjoy.

3. Enlist as much student help as possible in the layout process, either before, during, or after class. Emphasize participation rather than perfection because layout is rich with opportunities for skills other than language learning to come into play.

4. Prepare articles (i.e. compositions) in final form for publication as you go along, so an end-of-course publication will not require a last-minute rush.

5. Since the class publication projects are by and for the students, drawings made by students will certainly engage everyone. Cartoons, graphs, and humorous advertisements for fantasy products, as well as more serious illustrations are easily displayed, photocopied, or scanned for publications.

6. As opportunities develop in the life of your school or community, have students collect information on events, or have them interview other students and write brief reports of past or upcoming events for publication. You could also include other features, such as a horoscope, advice column, restaurant or movie reviews, or favorite recipes and holidays.

7. Be sure to allot some class time to reading and discussing each publication. Ask questions based on articles in the publication, work the crossword puzzle, fill in any cloze activities, and so on to get maximum pleasure from the final product.

What exactly is the Portfolio Project?

The portfolio project, which is begun in Unit 2 and continued in subsequent units, consists of a series of guided-practice and independent-practice writing tasks, each marked by a portfolio icon (shown here in the left margin).

Portfolio writing is to be distinguished from multi-draft writing. If the writing course were to be compared to a season of soccer games, portfolio writing would be akin to practice sessions while writing and publishing multi-draft compositions would be like the big games.

The portfolio project simply involves students collecting all their portfolio assignments in a folder or binder throughout the course. It recognizes the fact that students need to produce more writing than a teacher can ever "mark" and provides a writing routine that produces easy-to-do and easy-to-evaluate writing practice. The **guided-practice portfolio writing** is a series of structured tasks that help students turn out a half-page or page of prose in English on a daily basis. In the **independent-practice portfolio writing**, on the other hand, students are asked to write on topics without guidance as part of a weekly portfolio routine that teachers are encouraged to establish beginning in Unit 3. Appendix 3 provides more information and topics. We highly recommend that you customize the topics to suit the mood or events in your classroom, school, or community.

How should I decide what to do in class and what to assign for homework?

For best results, do most of the major multi-draft compositions in class and, as often as possible, write along with the students. Spending time in class on compositions emphasizes their importance, as does the teacher's participation as an individual. Both send the message that writing is something worth doing. In class, students cannot easily ignore or avoid doing writing, and the teacher can be certain of what students can do on their own in a given period of time.

For homework, students should routinely produce a half-page or more of text in English principally through portfolio practice assignments or the follow-up activities associated with the dictations. This controlled type of homework takes relatively little time, so students are more likely to do it. A student who will not go home and write a composition based on a class discussion *will* go home and rewrite a practice text previewed in class. The persistent practice pays off in both expanded vocabulary for writing and improved physical writing fluency with keyboarding or handwriting. Furthermore, this type of homework is easy for the teacher to mark. By correcting and returning it quickly, a teacher further encourages students to work outside class.

How is grammar handled?

From Writing to Composing is not a grammar book. The activities do not lead students through a progression of grammar points. Students encounter, simultaneously rather than sequentially, these four tenses: the simple present, the present continuous, the simple past and occasionally the present perfect. The greatest emphasis, however, is on the simple past. Students are expected to gain control of tenses as well as a miscellany of other grammar points through repeated exposure and practice rather than though explicit grammar lessons.

To make the best use of this book, be careful in early units not to get sidetracked by the frequent sentence structure and grammar mistakes students will make in their writing. Although a brief explanation of specific points is indeed necessary at times, resist the temptation to take a significant amount of class time in order to do a complete grammar review. Instead, move on to new writing and composing activities. The constant flow of new topics will keep students' attention focused on the real goal of writing and communicating meaning, while providing fresh opportunities to practice troublesome grammar points again and again.

It is also important to note the 23 file cards that appear throughout the book, some of which focus on sentence structure. Teachers can adjust the amount of time spent on sentence structure points, according to the needs of their students. Here is a list of the file cards and their locations in the book.

Features of a Letter, p. 5
Features of E-mail, p. 7
Capitalization and Punctuation, p. 12
Sentences, p. 12
Paragraphs, p. 16
Enumeration, p. 17
Format for a Student Paper, p. 20
Narration, p. 27
Compound Subjects, Verbs, and Sentences, p. 29
Formal Style, p. 42
Process, p. 57
Grouping Information, p. 69

Complex Sentences, p. 76
Fragments, Run-ons, and Comma Splices, p. 77
Chronology, p. 80
Sensory Details, p. 83
Classification, p. 92
Enumeration Signals, p. 102
Examples, p. 112
Anecdotes, p. 118
Essays, p. 122
Introductions, p. 126
Conclusions, p. 127

What is Appendix 1: The Mini-Handbook?

The Mini-Handbook is a tool to help teachers meet a wide range of possible student needs. It begins with the alphabet as the smallest building block of writing and moves to progressively larger elements, including words, phrases, sentence types, and paragraphs, and ends with mechanics issues, which are capitalization and punctuation. It is not intended to be comprehensive or a required part of the instructional program but rather to provide extra practice that may not be appropriate for all students and therefore was not included in the student pages.

My classes have 35 to 40 students, or more. How can I use *From Writing to Composing*?

The activities in this book have been used with classes of all sizes. Naturally, how activities are managed with a large class is somewhat different than with a small one. Here are some tips.

- A basic recommendation regarding the structured work, including the guided-practice portfolio writing, which makes up the bulk of the homework, is to check a lot of it orally in class. To keep students on their toes and doing their homework on a daily basis, collect and grade everyone's portfolio on a weekly or bi-weekly basis.

- With multi-draft compositions, always collect and read (but do not mark) everyone's first drafts. This is quick to do and will give you an overview of each person's problems and help you frame the subsequent activities so that they are relevant and useful to everyone. You will of course have to spend considerable time, on a frequent basis, editing and reacting to each person's second drafts and final compositions.

- In all types of writing, use pair and group work to the maximum to ensure that each person gets a lot of interaction time in each class session.

- To make sure you stay in touch with each person on a regular basis, interact with students in writing. Begin by customizing some of the independent-practice portfolio topics to suit your class, and then respond to student writing by adding a personalized dialog-journal response to their portfolio writing as often as time allows.

- If you and your students have access to e-mail, you can use it to stay in touch with your students and give them feedback on their writing.

Acknowledgements

Revising this textbook has been a long and demanding process that has occupied many evenings, weekends, and vacations, and we have many people to thank. First of all, we wish to acknowledge the useful feedback and suggestions from reviewers who read an early draft: Lia Plakans of The University of Iowa, Catherine Salin of Capital University, Susanne Linden Seidel of Nassau Community College, and Stephen Smollin of Korea University. In addition, we sincerely thank Patricia Jobe of The University of Texas at Austin, who not only reviewed the early draft but also pilot-tested the manuscript and sustained us with her enthusiastic support. We also want to thank some of the people who have worked so hard on our behalf to produce this book: Bernard Seal (commissioning editor) and Helen Lee (project editor) from Cambridge University Press; Jennifer Bixby, freelance development editor; and Don Williams, the compositor. Finally, we want to express our appreciation to our students who contributed both ideas and actual writing.

Carol wishes to acknowledge the help and support throughout the process from her dear friends, Ricky Fitzgerald and Liz Murphy. She also thanks all her colleagues at The University of Texas at Austin, and particularly Patricia Jobe, Letha McIntire, and Michael Smith, for their encouragement. Finally, she thanks her family, Edith King, Bryan and Jan King, and Geoffrey King, for their unwavering support.

Beverly expresses warm appreciation for understanding and encouragement to family members Gwen Ingram, Kevin Sladek, Will Sladek, and Katharina Hathaway. She also thanks colleagues Mildred Rugger and Janis Schiller at Texas State University-San Marcos and loyal friend Jan Rudnicki. Above all, she thanks her husband, Phil Sladek, for his empowering love and support from beginning to end.

Lastly, co-authors and dear friends, Carol and Bev, would like to give special thanks and acknowledgement to each other. Without the other, each would have given up long ago.

Part One

Getting Started

Dear Classmates

In this unit, you will get acquainted with your classmates. You will also learn the correct format for letters and e-mail, and you will practice writing and answering them.

1.1 Letters and e-mail

January 5, 2004

Dear Students,

Welcome to *From Writing to Composing*. We wrote this book to give you and your teacher a collection of interesting and useful activities. Together you and your teacher can use these activities to improve your writing in English. With practice, you will begin to write more fluently and confidently. Good luck and best wishes for a very productive course.

Sincerely,

Beverly & Carol

Beverly & Carol

From: Juan Silva <xyzjs@cool.com>
To: Carlos Garza <xyzcg@cool.com>
Date: Wednesday, January 14, 2004 3:49 PM
Subject: Hi!

Dear Carlos,

How's it going? How many classes do you have? I just started my classes yesterday, and I already have too much homework! I'm taking four courses, including writing. That's why I'm writing you in English. (I hope you understand my English! Ha, ha!) Write me soon. I want to hear all about your new life at college.

Best regards,
Juan

---

1 Read the letter and the e-mail message. Then answer these questions with a partner.

1 Who wrote the letter? Who wrote the e-mail message?

2 Do you ever write letters or e-mail in English?

3 Do you ever write letters or e-mail in your native language? If so, how often?

4 Do you write letters by hand, or do you type them?

5 Do you prefer to write letters or e-mail? Why?

2 Share your answers with the class.

1.2 A letter about a classmate

A Interviewing to get information for writing

1 Work with your class to write interview questions. The first one has been done for you as an example.

The Interview
1. Full name   Question: _What's your full name?_   Partner's answer: _____
2. Birthday   Question: _____   Partner's answer: _____
3. City, country   Question: _____   Partner's answer: _____
4. Occupation   Question: _____   Partner's answer: _____
5. Length of time here   Question: _____   Partner's answer: _____
6. Reason for studying English   Question: _____   Partner's answer: _____
7. Plans for the future   Question: _____   Partner's answer: _____
8. Free-time activities   Question: _____   Partner's answer: _____

2 Interview a partner, and write your partner's answers.

3 Introduce your partner to the class, using the information from the interview.

B Writing a letter

1 Write a letter about your partner to a family member. For your letter, use the framework in the box below. Choose the correct words, and add the missing information.

_____
(date)

Dear _____ ,

     I don't/doesn't/aren't *have much time to write now, but I want to*

say/said/saying *hello. I am very busy because I* am/is/are *starting my*

English class at _____ . *There* is/are _____ *students*
                (school)   (number)

in my class. Let me tell you about one of them.

_____ *is from* _____ . _____ *was*
  (full name)   (city/country)   (first name)

born on/in/at _____ . She/He *is* a/an _____ .
         (year)   (occupation)

_____ *has been here for* _____ *months. In the future,*
(first name)   (number)

she/he *plans to* _____ . _____ *and I will spend*
                          (first name)

_____ *hours together each week in this class. Maybe we will*
(number)

become good friends.

     I have to stop now. I hope you are doing well. Say hello to

_____ *for me. I miss you.*

                        Love,

                       _____
                          (signature)

---

2 Ask your partner to read your letter and tell you if the information is correct. Mark all necessary changes.

3 Write a final copy of the letter.

1.3 Features of a letter

1 Read the letter below. Label the following parts of the letter: *date, greeting, body, closing,* and *signature.*

2 Label the parts of the letter in 1.1 in the same way.

April 17, ____

Dear Karen,

 I am a new student in your writing class. I want to introduce myself. I am from Mexico. I was born on September 19, 1986, in Monterrey. I am a student. I have been living here since I was born. My mailing address is Av. Leon, Col. Juarez, Monterrey, Mexico. My phone number is 33-45-99. I don't have an e-mail address yet. I am studying English because I want to communicate better. In the future, I plan to travel to many countries. In my free time, I enjoy taking dance lessons, especially tap dancing, and reading about space travel.
 I am very happy to meet you. I hope this class will help me learn how to write better in English. Thanks for a great first class.

    Sincerely,

    Marco Reyes

_____

_____

_____

_____

_____

3 Read the file card below.

FEATURES OF A LETTER

Here are the features of a good letter:

Format
- A letter has five parts: date, greeting, body, closing, and signature.
- It ends with the writer's name (signature).

Content
- A letter focuses on the reader – in the beginning and again at the end.
- It does *not* begin with the writer's name, i.e., *not* "My name is . . ."
- It begins with a reason for writing and, therefore, a reason for reading.

4 Discuss whether the letter above has all the good features listed on the file card.

1.4 More letters

A Writing a letter to the teacher

1 Use the letter in 1.3 as a guide to write a letter about yourself to your teacher. Include some or all of the following information:

- Native country or language
- Birthday or age
- Occupation
- Address, including zip code or postal code
- Phone number, including area code

- E-mail address
- Reasons for studying English
- Plans for the future
- Free-time activities

2 Give the letter to your teacher to correct.

B Writing a letter to the class

1 Write a letter to your class by rewriting the letter that you wrote to your teacher in 1.4A. Because you are writing to a new audience, you may want to add or delete information. Begin your letter: "Dear Classmates."

2 Share your letter with your class by posting it in your classroom.

1.5 E-mail messages

A Reading e-mail messages

1 Read the e-mail messages between two students.

2 How is the format of the e-mail messages different from letter format?

From: "Sang Kim" <sk1022@cool.com>
Date: Tuesday, June 8, 2004 2:08 PM
To: "Maria Perez" <maria_perez@cool.com>
Cc: bev@cool.edu
Subject: Three More Facts about Me

Dear Maria,

I am very happy to have you as one of my classmates. I have many secrets to tell! Just kidding!

Let me tell you more about myself. The first new fact is that I have one younger brother who is studying in the United States. The second fact is that my wife is studying for her Ph.D. The third fact is that this is my second visit to the United States. I studied English for six months in Rhode Island, which is the smallest state in the United States.

That's all for now. Have a nice weekend. See you on Monday.

Sincerely,
Sang Kim

From: "Maria Perez" <maria_perez@cool.com>
Date: Tuesday, June 8, 2004 3:18 PM
To: "Sang Kim" <sk1022@cool.com>
Cc: bev@cool.edu
Subject: Re: Three More Facts about Me

Dear Sang,

Thank you for your e-mail. It is nice to meet you, too. I have one thing in common with you. I also lived in Rhode Island. I was a student at the Technical Community College for nine months. I lived in an American family's house, and I still write to them from time to time. Also, this is the third time I have visited the United States. The second time I was in Iowa for business, but it was only for ten days.

I hope you enjoy my e-mail. I hope I did not make a lot of mistakes. Take care!

Best regards,
Maria Perez

P.S. Have a good weekend!

B Talking about e-mail

1 Read the file card below.

FEATURES OF E-MAIL

E-mail (electronic mail) has these features:

Format
- It should have a title in the subject line.
- It begins with a greeting and ends with a closing and the writer's name.
- The "Cc" line can be used to send a copy of the message to another person.

Content
- The message is short and clear.
- E-mail is usually written in a more conversational style than a letter.
- School and business messages should have complete sentences, good grammar, and correct spelling.

2 Discuss whether the e-mail messages in 1.5A have all the good features listed in the file card.

C Exchanging e-mail with classmates

1. Put everyone's names and e-mail addresses in a hat. (To set up a free e-mail account, go to www.hotmail.com or www.yahoo.com.)

2. Draw the name of a classmate to e-mail.

3. Write an e-mail message to this person to tell three *more* things about yourself. Use the sample e-mail messages in 1.5A as a guide. (If you don't have an e-mail address, you can exchange letters instead.)

4. When you receive the e-mail from your classmate, answer it promptly, and include more information about yourself.

5. Use the Cc line to send a copy of your e-mail messages to your teacher.

Unit 2 Friends and Relatives

In this unit, you will write about people who are important to you. You will also make a portfolio for your writing and learn about the basics of capitalization, punctuation, and sentences.

2.1 Important people

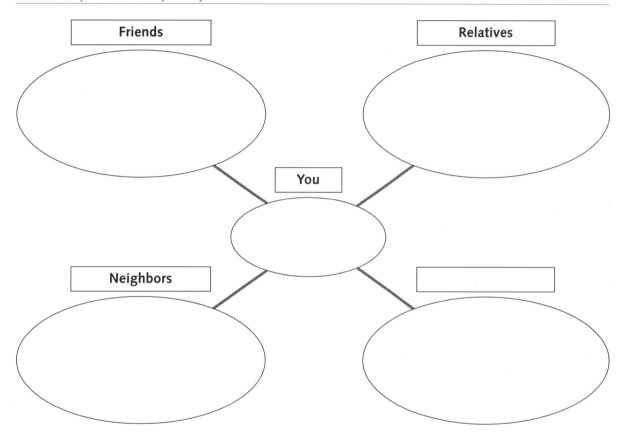

1 Think about people who are important to you. They can include friends, neighbors, close family members and other relatives, classmates, teammates, people at work, or others. Write their names in the circles in the diagram. You can add, rename, or delete circles if you want.

2 Talk about your diagram with a partner. Take turns asking and answering these questions.

1 Did you add, rename, or delete any circles? If so, which ones?

2 Where does each person live?

3 How often do you see or talk to each person?

4 Which people do you have photos of?

5 Which people do you send letters or e-mail messages to? How often do you write them?

2.2 Independent-practice writing

1 Choose a person from your diagram or from the box below to write about. Talk about your choice with your partner by asking and answering these questions.

   1 Which person did you choose?

   2 What is this person like?

   3 Why is this person important to you?

Important People

1 A good friend	6 Your mother or father
2 Your best friend	7 Your aunt
3 A childhood friend	8 Your favorite cousin
4 A special family friend	9 Your boss or a colleague
5 A brother or a sister	10 Your neighbor

---

2 Write about the person you chose.

   • Spend about 15–30 minutes writing.

   • Write 100–200 words.

   • Focus on your ideas.

   • Don't worry much about mistakes.

   • Save this independent-practice writing assignment.

2.3 The portfolio project

An important part of this course is the portfolio project, which will give you a lot of writing practice. You might compare writing for the portfolio project to practicing a sport before playing a big game. When you practice writing often, you will do better when you have to write something important.

A Thinking about writing practice

1 Work with a partner. Mark each statement *T* for True or *F* for False. Discuss your answers with the class.

   1 _____ You must practice often to learn to play soccer well.

   2 _____ You must practice writing a lot to learn to write well.

   3 _____ Doing a writing project, or long-term assignment, is a good way to get a lot of writing practice.

   4 _____ Sometimes you should focus on communicating your ideas, not on writing perfect sentences.

5 _____ The teacher must correct all of your writing practice for you to learn to write well.

6 _____ The best way for a teacher to evaluate your writing is to read your essay exam at the end of the course.

2 Discuss your answers with the class.

B Starting a portfolio

1 Buy an inexpensive folder or notebook with prongs or rings. See Appendix 3 page 146 for instructions on making your portfolio.

2 Put your paper from 2.2 in your folder. This is an example of **independent-practice portfolio writing**. In this type of writing, you should focus on communicating ideas clearly and writing efficiently.

3 Put the following letters from Unit 1 in the folder: the letter about your partner, the letter about yourself, and the letter to the class. These are examples of **guided-practice portfolio writing**. In guided practice, you are given some or all of the words or sentences needed to do the writing. You should focus on accuracy when you do guided-practice portfolio writing.

4 Keep all of your portfolio writing together in this folder. Do not remove any previous writing or throw anything away when you add new work. Your teacher will check your portfolio on a regular basis.

5 When you see the following symbol in the margin, it means that the writing can be added to your portfolio.

2.4 Introduction to capitalization and punctuation

A Can you read this?

1 Read the paragraph in the box.

> the portfolio project
>
> do you already have a collection of your writing many people do they keep diaries and journals during their life they want to write down their ideas and save their writing the portfolio project will help you save your writing from your writing course

2 Discuss these questions with your class.

1 Why is the paragraph hard to read?

2 Some basic components of writing are missing. Can you name them?

B Adding capitalization and punctuation

1 Read the file card. (See Mini-Handbook pages 139–41 for more on capitalization and punctuation.)

CAPITALIZATION AND PUNCTUATION

In English a **capital letter** is used for:
- The first word in a sentence.
- Proper names.
- Important words in a title.

The following **punctuation** ends a sentence:
- A period.
- A question mark.
- An exclamation point.

2 Rewrite the paragraph in 2.4A, adding capital letters and correct punctuation.

2.5 Introduction to sentences

A Talking about sentences, subjects, and verbs

1 Do you know what a sentence is? You might say it is a group of words beginning with a capital letter and ending with period, but a sentence is more than that. Read the file card below with your class. (See Mini-Handbook page 131 for more on sentences.)

SENTENCES

Sentences are groups of words that express a complete idea. They begin with a capital letter and end with a punctuation mark.

    Small dogs are good pets.
    Do you have any pets?
    My neighbor has fifteen cats!

Sentences have at least one subject and one verb.

        S   V
    My family has two dogs.

    V S V
    Do you like dogs?

      V   S
    There are several dogs in my neighborhood.

2 Read this paragraph that a student wrote about her family. She marked each subject with an *S* and each verb with a *V*. Count how many sentences she has in her paragraph, and put a number at the beginning of each sentence.

> My Family
>
>   ^S ^V   ^V   ^S
>
> Sometimes I feel homesick for my family. There are five people in my family.
>
> They are my father, mother, two older brothers, and myself. My father is a
>
> government official. He tells funny jokes, cooks delicious meals for the family, and
>
> grows vegetables in his garden. His jokes and his cooking are two of my favorite
>
> things. My mother is a nurse. She is outgoing, hardworking, and still curious about
>
> learning new things in her profession. She has recently changed jobs, and her new
>
> hospital is a very difficult place to work. I will write about my brothers another time.
>
> (100 words)

3 Answer these questions and discuss your answers with a partner.

    1 How many sentences are in her paragraph?

    2 Which sentence has one subject and three verbs?

    3 Which sentence has two subjects and one verb?

    4 How is sentence 2 different from the other sentences?

B Identifying subjects and verbs

1 Mark each underlined word with an *S* for subject or a *V* for verb.

> My Dog Shorty
>
>   At home in Mexico, <u>I</u> <u>have</u> a little dog. <u>She</u> <u>is</u> an important part of our family.
>
> <u>We</u> <u>call</u> her Shorty. <u>She</u> <u>is</u> a little fat, but <u>her shape</u> <u>is</u> very cute. <u>All my friends</u> <u>know</u>
>
> her name and <u>play</u> with her. <u>My father</u> sometimes <u>gets</u> angry with her because <u>she</u>
>
> <u>eats</u> plants in his garden. <u>His tomatoes</u> and <u>flowers</u> <u>are</u> her favorite snacks. <u>I</u> <u>would</u>
>
> <u>like</u> to pet Shorty right now.

2 Compare answers with a partner.

C Adding subjects and verbs

1 Some subjects and verbs are missing from this paragraph. Identify the missing words by writing an *S* for subject or a *V* for verb in the circles.

My Twin Brothers

Today I want to write about my two really wonderful older brothers. They ◯ twins and were born on Christmas Eve. ◯ are university students in Japan. One brother ◯ to a university in Osaka, and the other goes to a university in Kyoto. Therefore, they do not live at home with my family right now. They ◯ majoring in geography. This year ◯ will graduate from their universities and are thinking about graduate school. We ◯ usually in touch by e-mail, but I sent them a beautiful postcard last week. ◯ miss them very much and want to see them soon.

2 Rewrite the paragraph correctly.

3 When you are finished, put your paper in your portfolio.

D Identifying subjects and verbs in your writing

1 In 2.2 you wrote about an important person in your life. Reread your work. How many sentences did you write?

2 Mark the subjects and verbs in your sentences with an *S* and a *V*. If any are missing, add them.

Unit 3 Staying in Touch

In this unit, you will learn the structure of a paragraph and the correct format for a student paper. You will also do the first of five dictations in this book.

3.1 Enumeration dictation

A Talking about dictations

1 With your class, brainstorm about situations where it is sometimes necessary to write down things that you hear.

2 Discuss reasons why dictation is a good activity for learning a foreign language.

B Dictation, Version 1

This book uses dictations to help you develop your ability to write things down quickly and accurately and to improve your spelling and punctuation. The dictations will also help you understand paragraph organization, learn new vocabulary, and gain information about a variety of topics.

1 On a separate piece of paper, write the paragraph as your teacher dictates. Write the title in the center of the top line. Indent the first line of the paragraph. (The script for the teacher is in Appendix 2.)

2 Look at what you wrote, and answer these questions with your class.

  1 How many capital letters are there in the title?

  2 Did you indent the first sentence?

  3 How many sentences are there in the paragraph?

  4 Did you capitalize the first word of every sentence?

  5 Did you put a period at the end of every sentence?

  6 The last sentence uses an introductory word. Did you insert a comma after this word?

3 Compare your paragraph to the one on the next page. Check punctuation, capitalization, spelling, and format. Circle any errors.

Staying in Touch

People today have three good ways of staying in touch with friends and relatives. The first way is writing letters. The second way is making phone calls. The third way is sending e-mail messages. Therefore, there is really no technological reason for people not to communicate.

(46 words)

C Talking about the dictation

1 Discuss these questions about the topic of the dictation.

1 Which way of staying in touch is the most traditional? Which way is the newest?

2 Which way is the most expensive?

3 Which way do you prefer? Why?

4 Can you find a synonym (a word or phrase with the same or similar meaning) in the dictation for the following:

   a *family members*   d *electronic mail*

   b *stay in touch*   e *telephone*

   c *methods*

2 Discuss the structure of the dictation paragraph with your class.

1 This dictation is a paragraph, and it has several sentences on one topic. How many sentences does it have? What is the topic of the paragraph? (See Mini-Handbook page 133 for more information on gerunds.)

2 Read the *Paragraphs* file card below.

PARAGRAPHS

Good paragraphs in English consist of three to eight sentences on one topic.

Paragraphs usually have three parts:
- A **topic sentence**, usually at the beginning, which tells the main idea of the paragraph.
- Several **body sentences** in the middle, which give supporting information about the topic sentence.
- A **concluding sentence** at the end, which restates the topic sentence.

3 Underline the topic sentence in the dictation paragraph.

4 How many supporting sentences are there in the body of the dictation paragraph?

5 Underline the concluding sentence in the dictation paragraph.

D Enumeration

1 The supporting sentences in the body of a paragraph should be carefully organized. The type of organization in the dictation paragraph is called **enumeration** because it lists or numbers ways of staying in touch. How many ways of staying in touch are enumerated (listed, counted)?

2 Read the *Enumeration* file card below.

ENUMERATION

A good way to organize the supporting sentences in the body of a paragraph is to use enumeration.

Enumeration signal	Thing enumerated
The first	*way*
The second	*way*
The third	*way*

3 Circle the words in the dictation paragraph that signal enumeration.

E Adding support

A good enumeration paragraph supports each thing enumerated by adding examples, details, facts, or statistics. This supporting information helps the reader understand each idea.

1 The ideas in the dictation paragraph need support. Talk with a partner to decide where to add this supporting information to the dictation paragraph.

1 Telephoning is fast, and cell phones are making some long distance calls more economical.

2 People love getting personal letters.

3 This electronic method is both quick and convenient.

2 Rewrite the dictation paragraph, adding the supporting sentences. Use correct format as shown in the file card *Format for a Student Paper* on page 20.

3 When you are finished, put this guided practice in your portfolio.

F Self-correcting dictation

 Cover the phrase or sentence below each line. Write on the line as your teacher dictates. Then, when your teacher says to check, uncover the words, and check your writing.

1 _____

Staying in Touch

2 _____

Today, people have three good ways of communicating with friends and relatives.

3 _____

One quick, easy way is sending e-mail messages.

4 _____

Telephoning is the second way.

5 _____

The third way of staying in touch is writing letters.

6 _____

Therefore, there is really no technological reason for people not to stay in touch.

G Dictation, Version 2

1 Study Dictation, Version 1 carefully to prepare for Dictation, Version 2, which is a variation of Version 1.

 2 Write the Version 2 dictation paragraph as your teacher dictates. Give your paper to your teacher to check, or check your work as your teacher directs. (The script for the teacher is in Appendix 2.)

3.2 Student paper format

A Learning vocabulary about format

1 This *handwritten* paper by a student in an English class has good format. Identify the parts of this paper. Fill in the blanks with the words in the box.

blank line	lower left-hand corner	top line
bottom line	lower right-hand corner	upper left-hand corner
indentation	right margin	upper right-hand corner
left margin line	title	

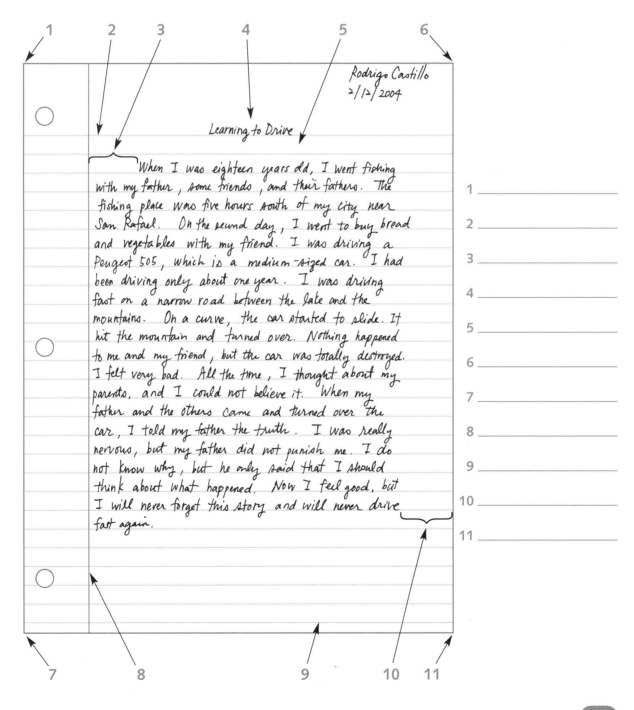

Rodrigo Castillo
2/12/2004

Learning to Drive

When I was eighteen years old, I went fishing with my father, some friends, and their fathers. The fishing place was five hours south of my city near San Rafael. On the second day, I went to buy bread and vegetables with my friend. I was driving a Peugeot 505, which is a medium-sized car. I had been driving only about one year. I was driving fast on a narrow road between the lake and the mountains. On a curve, the car started to slide. It hit the mountain and turned over. Nothing happened to me and my friend, but the car was totally destroyed. I felt very bad. All the time, I thought about my parents, and I could not believe it. When my father and the others came and turned over the car, I told my father the truth. I was really nervous, but my father did not punish me. I do not know why, but he only said that I should think about what happened. Now I feel good, but I will never forget this story and will never drive fast again.

1 _____
2 _____
3 _____
4 _____
5 _____
6 _____
7 _____
8 _____
9 _____
10 _____
11 _____

2 This is the *typed* version of the handwritten paper on page 19. It also has good format. With your class, identify the parts and features of this paper. Use the checklist shown on the *Format for a Student Paper* file card at the bottom of the page.

Rodrigo Castillo
2/12/2004

Learning to Drive

When I was eighteen years old, I went fishing with my father, some friends, and their fathers. The fishing place was five hours south of my city near San Rafael. On the second day, I went to buy bread and vegetables with my friend. I was driving a Peugeot 505, which is a medium-sized car. I had been driving only about one year. I was driving fast on a narrow road between the lake and the mountains. On a curve, the car started to slide. It hit the mountain and turned over. Nothing happened to me and my friend, but the car was totally destroyed. I felt very bad. All the time, I thought about my parents, and I could not believe it. When my father and the others came and turned over the car, I told my father the truth. I was really nervous, but my father did not punish me. I do not know why, but he only said that I should think about what happened. Now I feel good, but I will never forget this story and will never drive fast again.

FORMAT FOR A STUDENT PAPER

When typing a paragraph on the computer, use this format checklist as a guide.

___ **your name:** in the upper right-hand corner
___ **date:** below your name
___ **title:** centered, not in all caps, not underlined
___ **paragraph:** Indent the first line 0.5". Hit "Enter" only after the last line.
___ **line spacing:** double
___ **font:** standard type, such as Times New Roman
___ **font size:** 12
___ **plain text:** not bold or italics
___ **top and bottom margins:** 1"
___ **left and right margins:** 1.25"

B Reviewing vocabulary about format

1 Follow your teacher's instructions. Write numbers on the drawing below. The first number is written for you. (The script for the teacher is in Appendix 2.)

2 Fill in the blanks with the correct words.

1 The number 1 is in the upper left-hand _____ of the paper.

2 The number 4 is in the _____ right-hand corner of the page.

3 The number 10 is in the lower _____ corner.

4 The number 7 is in the _____ right-hand corner.

5 The number 3 is in the center of the _____ line.

6 The number 8 is in the middle of the _____ line.

7 The number 11 is on the left _____ line in the center of the page.

8 The number 6 is in the right margin in the _____ of the page.

3 Check your answers with a partner.

C Finding mistakes in format

1 This handwritten paper has many mistakes in format. Can you find at least nine mistakes and write them in the blanks? Use the vocabulary from 3.2A.

1 _____   4 _____   7 _____

2 _____   5 _____   8 _____

3 _____   6 _____   9 _____

When my family lived in another city, we had two experiences with robberies. One time someone broke into our car in front of our house and took some cds. We were upset and unhappy, but we did not call the police. It did not seem too important Another time a few weeks later, someone took our new camera and $55 from our house The person came in through a window when we were out of the house during the day. The camera was very expensive, and we did not have the money for another camera. We felt afraid and bought new locks.
Robberies were not only on T.V. They were real now.

Phillip Sladek
Phillip L. Sladek

2 This writer's typed paper also has mistakes in format. With a partner, make a list of at least fifteen mistakes in format.

NOT ONLY ON TV

When my family lived in another city, we had two
experiences with robberies.
One time someone broke into our car in front of our house
and took some CDs.
We were upset and unhappy, but we did not call the police.
It did not seem too important.
Another time a few weeks later, someone took our new
camera and $55 from our house.
The person came in through a window when we were out
of the house during the day.
The camera was very expensive, and we did not have the
money for another camera.
We felt afraid and bought new locks.
Robberies were not only on TV. They were real now.

Phillip L. Sladek   4/16/04

3 Check your list with the rest of the class. For help, refer to 3.2A (the sample paper and vocabulary) and the *Format for a Student Paper* file card on page 20.

4 Rewrite the paper using correct format.

5 Put this guided practice in your portfolio.

3.3 Independent-practice portfolio writing

1. Work with a partner or small group. Talk about the topics in the box.

2. Choose a topic from the box to write about in class or as homework. Focus on communicating your ideas. Do not worry about mistakes while you are writing, but be sure to reread and edit when you finish.

   • Use good format and paragraph structure.

   • Spend 15–30 minutes writing.

   • Write 100–200 words.

Topics

Thinking about staying in touch

1 Your favorite way of staying in touch with friends
2 Your opinion about cell phones
3 Your experience with instant messaging

Looking inside and outside yourself

4 Your hopes for the future
5 A special event in your school or city
6 A topic from the list on page 148

---

3. When you are finished, add your work to your portfolio.

Unit 4 Sharing Stories

> In this unit, you will read and rewrite a dramatic story, learn about the composing process, and write your own exciting story.

4.1 Talking about stories

1 Discuss these questions with a partner.

 1 How are these people sharing stories? How do you share stories with your family and friends?

 2 What was your favorite story as a child? Why?

 3 What is the top story in the news right now?

 4 What interesting or unusual story have you heard or read recently?

2 Share your answers with the class.

4.2 Writing a story

A Introduction to the story

1 Look at the pictures below, and listen while your teacher tells you the story.

2 Work with a partner or small group. Read the sentences, and match each one with picture A, B, C, or D. Write the letter of the picture in the blank.

_____ 1 The bank manager gives the woman a reward.

_____ 2 The woman begins to make a deposit and cash a check.

_____ 3 She stops him.

_____ 4 The man slowly walks to a window.

_____ 5 A woman and her grandson are in the bank.

_____ 6 She hits him hard with her umbrella.

_____ 7 He gives the boy seven balloons.

_____ 8 In the end, everyone is happy except the robber.

_____ 9 He gets two bags of money from her.

_____ 10 Then a man with a hat walks in.

_____ 11 He starts to run away.

_____ 12 A crowd watches.

_____ 13 He suddenly pulls out a gun.

_____ 14 The woman has a handbag and an umbrella on her arm.

_____ 15 It is an ordinary day at the First National Bank.

_____ 16 She looks very happy.

_____ 17 The boy has a balloon on a string.

_____ 18 A policeman immediately takes the robber away.

_____ 19 The woman quickly starts to run after him.

_____ 20 The boy also has a smile on his face.

_____ 21 He gives the teller a note.

3 With a partner, decide which sentence about picture A is the first sentence in the story. Write *A-1* in the blank beside it. Label the second sentence *A-2*, and so on. Continue with the other pictures.

4 Check your answers with another pair of students and then the class.

B Writing the story

1 Read the file card below.

NARRATION

Telling a story is called narration.
- Narration usually uses chronological order. This means that the sentences in a story are presented in the order in which the events happen.
- Writers usually use the simple past tense to tell a story.
- Writers may sometimes use the simple present tense to tell a story.

2 Write the sentences from 4.2A in chronological order to tell the story.
- Use correct paragraph format (see page 20).
- Title your paragraph "An Unsuccessful Crime."

C Telling a story using the past tense

Writers sometimes use the simple present tense to tell stories. In these cases, it is called the historical present tense and helps make stories seem immediate and dramatic. The story you wrote in 4.2B is in the historical present tense. Another verb tense that writers often use to tell stories is the simple past tense.

1 With a partner, practice reading "An Unsuccessful Crime" in the simple past tense, using the verbs listed below. Take turns reading aloud, sentence by sentence. Do *not* write the verbs in the blanks.

An Unsuccessful Crime

(1)It ___ an ordinary day at the First National Bank. (2)A woman and her grandson ___ in the bank. (3)The woman ___ a handbag and an umbrella on her arm. (4)The boy ___ a balloon on a string. (5)The woman ___ to make a deposit and cash a check. (6)Then a man with a hat ___ in. (7)The man slowly ___ to a window. (8)He suddenly ___ out a gun. (9)He ___ the teller a note. (10)He ___ two bags of money from her. (11)He ___ to run away. (12)The woman quickly ___ to run after him. (13)She ___ him hard with her umbrella. (14)She ___ him. (15)A policeman immediately ___ the robber away. (16)A crowd ___. (17)The bank manager ___ the woman a reward. (18)She ___ very happy. (19)He ___ the boy seven balloons. (20)The boy also ___ a smile on his face. (21)In the end, everyone ___ happy except the robber.

1 was	8 pulled	15 took
2 were	9 gave	16 watched
3 had	10 got	17 gave
4 had	11 started	18 looked
5 began	12 started	19 gave
6 walked	13 hit	20 had
7 walked	14 stopped	21 was

2 With a partner, practice telling the story without looking at the list of verbs. Partner A covers the list of verbs and reads the story. Partner B checks by looking at the list of verbs.

3 Switch roles. Partner B covers the list of verbs and reads the story. Partner A checks by looking at the list of verbs.

4 Take turns until each partner can read all sentences correctly and easily.

5 Look back at the paragraph you wrote in 4.2B. With books closed, underline the verbs in the story, and write the simple past tense form above each verb.

6 Check your answers against the list of verbs in C1.

D Using compound subjects, verbs, and sentences

1 Read the file card.

COMPOUND SUBJECTS, VERBS, AND SENTENCES

You can make your writing smoother by using conjunctions such as *and*, *but*, and *so* to make compound subjects and verbs or compound sentences.

Compound subjects using *and*:
A boy walked to the park. His dog walked, too.
A boy *and* his dog walked to the park.

Compound verbs using *and*:
He walked in the kitchen. He went to the refrigerator.
He walked in the kitchen *and* went to the refrigerator.

Compound sentences using *and*, *but*, or *so* and a comma:
The glass started to fall. The man caught it.
The glass started to fall, *but* the man caught it.

2 Combine these sentence pairs from the story. Use *and*, *but*, or *so*. (See Mini-Handbook pages 135–6 for more on simple and compound sentences.)

1 The man walked slowly to a window.
He suddenly pulled out a gun.

The man walked slowly to a window and suddenly pulled out a gun.

2 He gave the teller a note.
He got two bags of money from her.

3 She hit him hard with her umbrella.
She stopped him.

4 The woman had a handbag and an umbrella on her arm.
The boy had a balloon on a string.

5 He started to run away.
The woman quickly started to run after him.

6 A policeman immediately took the robber away.
A crowd watched.

7 The bank manager gave the woman a reward.
She looked very happy.

8 He gave the boy seven balloons.
The boy had a smile on his face.

E Adding details

Adding details makes a story more interesting, clearer, and more complete. One way of adding details is to use descriptive adjectives. Another way is to add information.

1 Work with a partner to think of as many places as possible to use each adjective below in the story you wrote in 4.2B. Then choose the best place for each one.

big	heavy	old
black-and-white	little	teller's
elderly	long	young
famous	new	

2 Answer these questions, and work with a partner to find good places to add this new information to the story.

  1 How do you think the boy feels when he sees the man's picture on the wall?

  2 Where do you think the policeman takes the robber?

3 Now rewrite the story from 4.2B.

  • Add the adjectives and information from steps 1 and 2.

  • Use the simple past tense.

  • Use the sentences you wrote from 4.2D.

4 When you are finished, put the story in your portfolio.

4.3 Revising and editing

A Checking for a topic sentence

A topic sentence is usually at the beginning of a paragraph. In a story or narrative paragraph, however, a topic sentence containing the main idea is sometimes at the end and tells the moral of the story. The moral tells the meaning, point, or lesson of a story. (See Mini-Handbook page 138 for more on the position of topic sentences in a paragraph.)

1 Read the story in the box.

> Quick Action
>
> It was an ordinary day at the First National Bank. Everything seemed normal. An elderly woman and her grandson were in the bank. The woman had an old handbag and a new umbrella on her arm, and the little boy had a balloon on a long string. The woman began to make a deposit and cash a check. Then a man with a black-and-white hat walked in. The little boy saw the man's picture on the wall and began to feel afraid. The man slowly walked to a teller's window and suddenly pulled out a big gun. He gave the teller a note and got two heavy bags of money from her. He started to run away, but the woman quickly started to run after him. She hit him hard with her umbrella and stopped him! A young policeman immediately took the famous robber away to jail, and a crowd watched. The bank manager gave the woman a reward, so she looked very happy. He gave the boy seven balloons, so the boy also had a big smile on his face. In the end, everyone was happy except the robber. In this incident, quick action by an ordinary person stopped a crime.

2 Discuss these questions with a partner and your class.

1 How are "Quick Action" and the story you wrote in 4.2E different?

2 Which story presents the main idea more clearly?

3 Find and underline the topic sentence of "Quick Action."

B Changing the facts

A writer can vary a story by changing some of the facts. For example, a writer can change the gender of the characters. Changes in gender require changes in pronouns and perhaps changes in other details such as clothing.

1 Rewrite the story from 4.2E using these facts:
- A *man* and his *granddaughter* are at the bank.
- The robber is a *woman.*

2 When you are finished, put your paper in your portfolio.

C Using editing symbols

Editing symbols help writers, editors, teachers, and students communicate about making corrections. You will need to understand these editing symbols when you correct your writing. (The editing symbols are explained in Appendix 4 on page 149.)

Rewrite the sentences below, using the editing symbols as a guide to make corrections.

1 A woman and his grandson in the bank.

2 Was an ordinary day to the bank.

3 Everyone were happy except ∅ the robber.

sv
agr

4 The rober pulled out gun.

sp *art.*

5 The boy, was also smiling, too.

p *rep*

6 The woman had a hand bag and umbrella on your arm.

pro
agr

7 The boy liked very much the ballon.

sp

8 The robbery happen at the First national bank yesterday.

vt *c* *c*

9 The robber hat was black and white.

poss *p*

10 He gaves the boy some balloon.

wf *#*

4.4 Letters and e-mail

A Talking about point of view

1 Discuss how each of the following people felt during the unsuccessful bank robbery in 4.2.

1 the elderly woman

2 the bank teller

3 the bank robber

4 a person who saw the robbery

2 Imagine it is the next day. The robbery was the top story in the evening news. Discuss how each of these people feels today.

B Salutations and closings

1 Imagine that each of the four people listed above is going to write a letter or e-mail. Who would each person write to? Would the letter or e-mail be formal or informal?

2 Here are some common salutations for letters and e-mail. Write *F* if it is a formal salutation or *I* if it is an informal salutation.

_____ 1 Dear Martin,

_____ 2 Dear Officer Reed:

_____ 3 Dear Sir:

_____ 4 Hi Fred,

_____ 5 Dear Ms. Jones:

_____ 6 Dear Mr. Wilson:

_____ 7 Martha,

3 Here are some common closings for letters and e-mail. Write *F* if it is a formal closing or *I* if it is an informal closing.

_____ 1 Sincerely,

_____ 2 Warmly,

_____ 3 Best regards,

_____ 4 Love,

_____ 5 Yours sincerely,

_____ 6 Fondly,

_____ 7 Best,

C Writing a letter or e-mail

1 Work with your class, and write the first sentence of each letter or e-mail written by the following people.

   1 The elderly woman tells the story in a letter to her friend.

   2 The bank teller tells the story in an e-mail to her sister.

   3 The bank robber tells the story in a letter to his lawyer.

   4 You write a statement for the police in an e-mail, telling what you saw.

2 Take the point of view of one of the people above. Continue writing the letter or e-mail you started with your class. Use an appropriate salutation and closing from 4.4B.

3 When you are finished, add your paper to your portfolio.

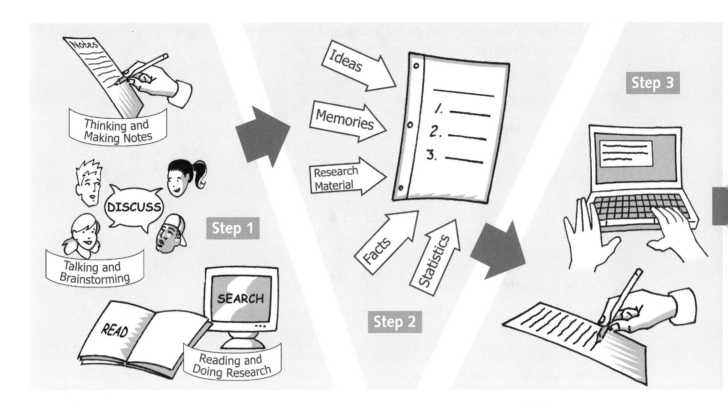

4.5 Your story and the composing process

Good writers use a process approach when they compose. In a process approach, you develop and revise a piece several times, going through different steps. In this assignment, you and your teacher will follow a process approach to write an exciting or important personal experience story.

Step 1: Brainstorm and collect ideas.

⬤ Have you ever been in an emergency situation, such as a robbery, an accident, a fire, or a medical emergency? Have you had an exciting experience, such as winning a championship? Has someone in your family? Briefly describe the situation in a small group.

⬤ Listen to your teacher tell a story about a personal experience. Listen for past tense verbs.

Step 2: Organize your ideas and plan your writing.

⬤ Most stories are presented in chronological order. Review the *Narration* file card on page 27.

⬤ Plan and organize your writing. Make a list of three or four main events of your story. Put them in chronological order. Use past tense verbs.

Step 3: Write a first draft.

⬤ Write a first draft of your story.

  • Write one paragraph.

  • Write for 15 minutes, including as many details as possible.

  • Don't worry about mistakes.

  • Leave a blank or use a word from your language if you can't think of the word in English.

Reread your first draft and then give it to your teacher, who will read it and write some questions about it. The questions will help you add more information and details in Step 4.

Step 4: Revise the first draft.

Add details. Read the first draft of your teacher's story. With your class, take turns asking questions about your teacher's story to get more information. Discuss where these details can be added to your teacher's first draft.

Read the questions your teacher has written about your first draft. Write your answers and decide where the new information can be added.

Add a topic sentence. Help your teacher write or improve his or her topic sentence. Use the teacher's answers to these two questions to understand the main idea and write the topic sentence.

• Why is this story important to you?

• How did this experience change you?

With a partner, discuss the main idea of your stories by asking the same questions as above. Now, write or improve your topic sentence.

Add a title. With your class, brainstorm titles for your teacher's story. Choose the best one.

Brainstorm titles for your story. Choose the best one.

Step 5: Write your second draft.

Help your teacher write a second draft by adding details, a topic sentence, and a good title.

Revise and rewrite your story. Add the supporting details (such as adjectives and information), the topic sentence, and the new title you wrote in Step 4.

Give your first and second drafts to your teacher.

Step 6: Edit and proofread your writing.

1 Look at the editing symbols marked on your second draft by your teacher. (For a review of editing symbols, turn to Appendix 4 on page 149.)

2 Review correct paper format by turning to pages 19 and 20.

3 Write your final draft. Proofread your writing by using this editing checklist.

> ___ Use correct paragraph format, with first line indented.
>
> ___ Begin sentences and proper names with a capital letter.
>
> ___ Check for a subject and verb in every sentence.
>
> ___ Put correct punctuation at the end of every sentence.
>
> ___ Include at least one compound sentence, using *and*, *so*, or *but*.

Step 7: Publish and share your final draft.

Share your story with your classmates. You can read stories aloud in small groups or display them in your classroom so that everyone can walk around and read them. You may also publish some or all of the stories as part of a class publication project. (Unit 6 describes several types of class publications.)

4.6 Thinking about the composing process

The composing process is much more than writing something just one time. In section 4.5, you went through the seven steps of the composing process. You will use this process in the writing activities in this book, as well as in other courses, so it is important to review the steps.

1 You completed seven steps in the composing process in 4.5. Draw a line to match each step with its name.

Step 1	a Revising the first draft
Step 2	b Brainstorming and collecting ideas
Step 3	c Writing a second draft
Step 4	d Editing and proofreading
Step 5	e Writing a first draft
Step 6	f Publishing and sharing your work
Step 7	g Organizing and planning

2 Look at the picture of Step 1 in the composing process on page 34. It shows several possible ways of getting ideas. Discuss which way(s) you used in this unit.

3 The picture of Step 4 on page 35 lists many good ways of revising. Discuss which way(s) you used in this unit.

4 The picture of Step 7 on page 35 shows two possible ways of sharing your writing with others. Discuss which way(s) your class used in this unit.

4.7 Independent-practice portfolio writing

1 Work with a partner or small group. Talk about the topics in the box.

2 Choose a topic from the box to write about in class or as homework. Focus on communicating your ideas. Do not worry about mistakes while you are writing, but be sure to reread and edit when you finish.

- Use good format and paragraph structure.
- Spend 15–30 minutes writing.
- Write 100–200 words.

Topics

More personal stories
1 An experience you want to forget
2 Something funny you did as a child

Looking inside and outside yourself
3 Your favorite time of the year
4 Something in the news
5 A topic from the list on page 148

---

3 When you are finished, add your work to your portfolio.

Unit 5 Three Good Ways

In this unit, you will learn about formal style and write a paragraph using this style.

5.1 Three ways of writing

One-step writing

Timed writing

Multi-draft writing

1 Look carefully at the three diagrams showing three ways of writing. Then answer these questions with your class.

1 Which way do you use when you are on vacation and write to a friend?

2 Which way do you use when you write a research paper for a class?

3 Which way do you use when you write a half-hour essay in an exam for admission to a university English program?

2 Write down another situation when it would be appropriate to use each way of writing. Share your ideas with the class.

1 One-step writing: _____

2 Timed writing: _____

3 Multi-draft writing: _____

5.2 Independent-practice portfolio writing

1 Work with a partner or small group. Talk about the topics in the box.

 2 Choose a topic from the box to write about in class or as homework. Focus on communicating your ideas. Do not worry about mistakes while you are writing, but be sure to reread and edit when you finish.

• Use good format and paragraph structure.

• Spend 15–30 minutes writing.

• Write 100–200 words.

Topics

Feelings

1 Do you like to write in your language? Why or why not?

2 Do you like to write in English? Why or why not?

3 Do you think you are a good writer? Why or why not?

Situations

4 In what situations do you write? For example, do you write at work or at home? What do you write there?

5 Which situations do you like to write in? Why?

6 Which situations do you dislike? Why?

Preferences

7 Where do you prefer to write?

8 Do you prefer to write with a computer or by hand? Why?

9 When do you prefer to write?

Process of writing

10 How do you get ready to write? Do you prepare a cup of tea? Do you take a walk?

11 Do you ever have trouble thinking of what to write? If so, what do you do?

12 What steps do you follow when you write in your language and in English? Which steps are easier? Which are harder?

---

 3 When you are finished, add your work to your portfolio.

5.3 Reading and editing

A Analyzing a paragraph

1 Read the paragraph in the box aloud with your teacher or a partner.

> Ways of Writing
>
> People have three good ways of writing. The first way is writing only one quick draft. People on vacation use this way when they write post cards to friends and relatives. The second way is planning, writing, revising, and editing several careful drafts. People use this way when they write something important. They usually get feedback from other people during the process. The third way is writing carefully in a timed situation, without help or feedback. People use this way during tests when they have to complete all the steps of the process in a short amount of time. All three ways of writing are useful if people use them in the appropriate situations.

2 Discuss the paragraph with your class.

1 How many ways of writing are explained in the paragraph?

2 What are these ways?

3 Which way probably includes the most planning time? The least planning time?

4 Which way allows writers to make the most changes before they finish?

5 Which way allows writers to check their writing carefully after they finish?

6 Which way did you use in Unit 4 when you wrote your personal story?

3 Analyze the structure of the paragraph.

1 Underline the topic sentence in the paragraph.

2 Circle the words in the paragraph that signal enumeration of the ways.

3 Underline the concluding sentence in the paragraph.

B Editing practice

Rewrite the sentences correctly, using the editing symbols as a guide. (The editing symbols are explained in Appendix 4 on page 149.)

1 People have three good ways of writing ^{p}

2 $^{art.}$ first way is write ^{wf} only one quick draft.

3 $^{art.}$ second way is planning, write ^{wf}, revising, and editing several carefully ^{wf} draft $^{\#}$.

4 People uses $^{sv\ agr}$ ⃝ way when ⃝^{s} write something important ^{p}

5 $^{art.}$ third way is write ^{wf} careful ^{wf} in a timed situaton ^{sp}, without help or feedback.

6 All three way $^{\#}$ of writing ⃝^{v} useful if people use ⃝ in the appropriate situations.

5.4 Introduction to outlines and diagrams

Outlining is a good way to see the structure of a paragraph when planning to write or while reading. A diagram is another useful way to see the structure of a paragraph.

A Writing an outline

1 Look at this outline of the paragraph "Ways of Writing." Finish the outline by filling in the blanks with words from the paragraph.

Ways of Writing

Topic: Three _____ ways of _____

   A. Writing _____ quickly

   B. Writing several drafts _____

   C. Writing carefully in a _____ amount of time

2 Read the paragraph below. Write an outline of the paragraph on a piece of paper.

Ways of Writing to Friends and Relatives

    People have three useful ways of writing to friends and relatives. The first way is writing letters by hand. People use handwriting when they want to be personal. They use it for thank-you notes and cards for special occasions. The second way is writing e-mail messages. People use this way because it is fast, convenient, and inexpensive. It is especially helpful when people are in different time zones. The third way is writing instant messages. People use this way for fun and for quick questions when they are working at a computer. It makes time at the computer seem less lonely. All three ways of writing to friends and relatives are very useful in the appropriate situations.

B Making a diagram of ideas

1 Look at this diagram of the ideas in the paragraph "Ways of Writing." This diagram uses boxes and lines to show the relationship of the main idea to the supporting ideas of the paragraph.

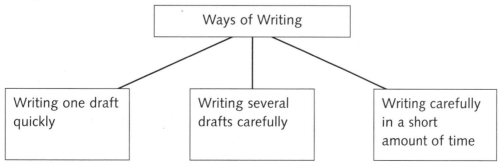

2 Complete this diagram with ideas in the paragraph "Ways of Writing to Friends and Relatives" in 5.4A.

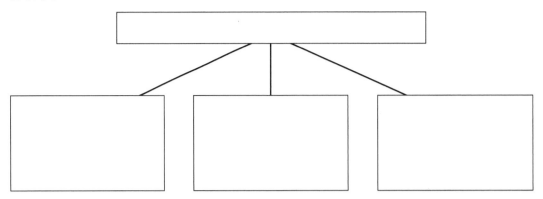

5.5 Introduction to formal style

A Comparing paragraphs

1 Work with a partner. Discuss in what ways the paragraph in the box below is different from the paragraph in 5.3A.

2 Share your ideas with your class, and list the differences.

> **Ways of writing**
>
> We've got several good ways of writing. The first way is that I can write one quick draft.
> If there's time, you can plan, write, revise and edit several careful drafts.
> Also, in a timed situation, when you write carefully, without help or feedback.
> In my opinion, all three ways of writing are useful if I use them in the appropriate situations.

B Discussing formal style

1 Work with a partner. Read the file card below, and decide which paragraph uses formal style: the one in 5.3A or in 5.5A?

> ### FORMAL STYLE
>
> Formal style is usually used in academic and professional writing.
>
> Here are four characteristics of formal writing:
> - It is carefully organized.
> - It has correct paragraph format. (See the *Paragraphs* file card on page 16.)
> - It is usually written in third person (*they, it, he,* or *she*). It avoids or limits the use of first and second person pronouns (*I, you, we, my,* and *our*).
> - It has no contractions, such as *don't* or *can't.*

2 Work with a partner. Read each situation, and write *F* for formal style and *I* for informal style.

1 _____ You take a phone call for your roommate and write a quick message to your roommate.

2 _____ You write the essay part of the TOEFL.

3 _____ You write a report for your department manager at work.

4 _____ You write an e-mail message to your cousin.

5 _____ You write an e-mail message to your former professor asking for a recommendation letter.

6 _____ You write a 30-minute essay in a class exam.

7 _____ You write your English grammar homework.

8 _____ You write an independent-practice assignment for your portfolio.

5.6 Formal style paragraph

A Getting ideas

1 Look at the writing topics in the box. Work with a partner. Add more possible topics.

> Three ways of making new friends
> Three ways of getting rid of unwanted visitors
> Three ways of getting over a broken heart
> Three ways of celebrating a birthday
> Three ways of sleeping in class
> Three ways of quitting smoking
>
> _____
> _____
> _____
> _____

2 With your partner, share your best ideas with the class.

B Stating an opinion

1 Reread the paragraph "Ways of Writing" in 5.3A, which gives three good ways of writing. The writer used the adjective *good* to express an opinion.

People have three good ways of writing.

2 Read the adjectives in the box. Write three more adjectives that express an opinion.

quick	easy	stupid	boring	dangerous
humorous	modern	successful	polite	inexpensive

_____   _____   _____

3 With a partner, practice stating opinions by combining the adjectives in the box with the topics in 5.6A.

Example:
There are three easy ways of getting over a broken heart.

C Planning your paragraph

1 Choose a topic to write about. Fill in the outline below with your topic, an opinion adjective, and three ways of doing this thing.

> **Topic:** Three _____ ways of _____
>
> A. _____
>
> B. _____
>
> C. _____

2 Give your outline to your teacher to check.

D Writing the first draft

1 Write one paragraph about your topic, using your outline and the enumeration signals on the *Enumeration* file card on page 17.

- Use formal style.
- Write for 15 minutes.
- Don't worry about mistakes or vocabulary.
- Leave a blank or use a word from your own language if you can't think of the word in English.

2 Read your paragraph. Add or change anything you wish.

E Using feedback to revise

1. Exchange first drafts with a partner. Read your partner's draft to see if your partner used formal style. Answer these questions by writing *Y* for yes or *N* for no in each blank.

    _____ 1 Does the paragraph have a topic sentence?

    _____ 2 Does it have clear enumeration signals?

    _____ 3 Does it have a concluding sentence?

    _____ 4 Does the paragraph have correct format like the example on page 20?

    _____ 5 Is the paragraph written using only third person pronouns?

    _____ 6 Does the paragraph avoid contractions?

2. Return your partner's paper. Discuss your answers to questions 1–6.

3. Revise your paper, according to your partner's feedback.

4. Write your second draft, adding an interesting title.

5. Give your teacher your outline, first draft, and second draft for additional revising and editing feedback.

F Editing and writing the final draft

1. Work with a partner. Look carefully at your teacher's revising and editing suggestions marked on your second draft. Explain to your partner how you will correct the mistakes. (For a review of editing symbols, turn to Appendix 4 on page 149.)

2. Write the final draft of your paragraph in class or on a computer, making all the changes that are marked.

G Sharing final drafts

Share your paper with others by publishing it in a class newspaper or magazine, posting it on a class Web site, or putting it in a wall display.

Unit 6 Class Publication

In this unit, you will get acquainted with newspapers and Web sites, start planning your class publication, and make a crossword puzzle for your publication.

6.1 Types of publications

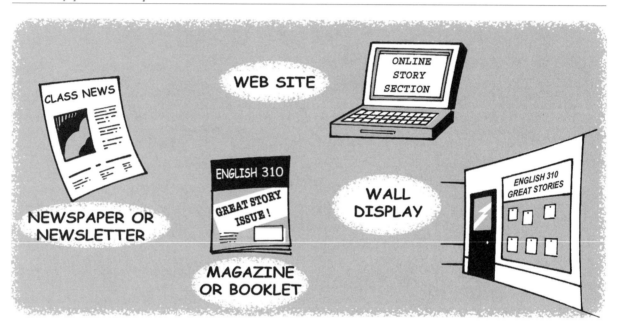

1 Look at the illustration with the class. Identify the different types of publications.

2 Discuss these questions with your class.

1 What do these publications have in common? How are they different?

2 Why do people, companies, schools, and other organizations make publications, such as newspapers, newsletters, magazines, booklets, Web sites, and wall displays?

3 Have you ever had any experience making a publication? If so, tell about it.

6.2 Newspapers

A Getting acquainted with newspapers

1 Discuss these questions with your class.

1 Do you read a newspaper in your native language? If so, which one? Why? How often?

2 Do you read a newspaper in English? If so, how often? Which paper? Why?

3 Which parts of the newspaper do you like to read? What types of articles and columns do you like?

2 Work with a partner or small group. Look at a recent English-language newspaper, and answer the following questions on a separate piece of paper.

Newspaper Questions

1 What is the name of the newspaper? What is the date? How much did it cost?

2 How many articles are on the front page? What is one of the headlines?

3 Where is the index? What types of things are listed in the index?

4 Is the newspaper divided into sections? If so, what are the names of the sections?

5 Can you find an article about international news? If so, where?

6 Where are the articles about local news?

7 Can you find an article about a robbery or other dramatic event? If so, where?

8 Where is the weather report?

9 Find an editorial. How is an editorial different from other newspaper articles?

10 Is there an advice column? If so, where?

11 Can you find a cartoon? If so, where? Are there any comic strips? If so, where?

12 Is there a graph or table? If so, where?

13 Where are the classified ads? What do they advertise?

14 What other kinds of ads are there?

15 Is there a horoscope? Is there a crossword puzzle? If so, where are they?

B Making a newspaper display

Work with a small group. Make a display about newspapers for your classroom. For the display, cut out an example from the newspaper of each item listed below. Put the items on a big sheet of paper, and label each one.

masthead of the paper	classified ad	crossword puzzle
advice column	advertisement	cartoon
article about local news	index	comic strip
weather report	editorial	headline
graph or table		

C Looking at a class newspaper

Look at the two-page class newspaper on pages 48–9. Work with a partner to find as many items from the list above as you can.

MEET LEVEL 2A

From Staff Reporters

The Level 2A class this spring is interesting and cooperative. The class consists of sixteen students: ten females and six males. They come from eight countries in Asia, Africa, America, and Europe. They speak the following native languages: Arabic, Chinese, Greek, Korean, Spanish, and Tigre. In their countries, they had various occupations including hair stylist, student, electrical technician, and driver. The students range in age from 20 to 41 years. The average age is 24.6 years. Six of the students are married. Three students live alone. The others live with their spouses and/or relatives. According to the teachers of the class, these students study hard and get along well. The teachers said, "It is really a pleasure to teach this group of varied people who work together well."

———•———

BLACK SKY

By Ana Nogueira

Last semester when I lived in Texas, I had a scary experience. It happened on the Friday night before spring break. The sky was dark, and the clouds were moving very quickly. I turned on the TV and listened to the weather channel. The newscaster was warning about a tornado near the lake. I was scared because I had never seen a tornado before. Suddenly, it began to rain pieces of ice, or hail. I began to be really scared. The hail was hitting my windows, so I went into the bathroom and waited for the storm to finish. I heard hours later that the tornado hit a few blocks from my house. It didn't cause any damage, but I know tornadoes are really dangerous. I didn't have real experience with a tornado before, and I was not prepared for it. Now I'm sure it is a good idea to listen to a weather report if it looks like a bad storm. I hope I don't have another experience like that.

LEVEL TWO AT MET AND PARK

From Staff Reporters

Review grammar while you get the news! Read and fill in the missing past-tense verbs.

Nine students and two teachers from Level 2A _____ an enjoyable day at the Metropolitan Museum and Central Park on May 22. Together they _____ the train to the Met, which is big and beautiful. First, they _____ at Greek statues and French art. Next, they _____ through the Chinese garden and _____ the Chinese students many questions about the things there. After that, they _____ the museum and walked to Central Park for a picnic. They _____ Colombian rice, American meat loaf, Cantonese tarts, and Japanese candy. Then, everybody sang and _____ games with a small ball. The students said that the day _____ fun because they saw wonderful art, shared ideas, _____ different styles of food, and spent relaxing time together outside of class.

———•———

AN AFRAID NIGHT

By Xiao-He Zhao

When I had just come to New York, I was not afraid when I walked home at night. One thing happened to my good friend to change me. One night, my good friend was going home after work. She was walking on the sidewalk. There were no people or cars in the street. Suddenly, a tall man jumped out of a doorway near her. He pulled out a sharp knife. He took her new handbag and expensive watch. He left. My friend did not say anything because she was very afraid. She lost a watch that cost $200 and $50 in money. After that, my friend didn't walk on the sidewalk at night. She bought a car to drive home. When my friend told me this dangerous thing, I was very afraid. Now I don't walk home at night. I'm very careful at night.

Answers for "What's My City" on page 2: 1.B, 2.C, and 3.A

TODAY'S WEATHER

- Clear, sunny skies
- Daytime high: 75°F
- Low tonight: 60°F

P.S. To enjoy today's weather, Go to El Valle, Colombia, in June.

Reporter: Edilma Torres

WHAT'S MY CITY?

Reporters: Nuo Cen, Michael Damianou, Chong Hak Kong
(answers at bottom of page 1)

Test your knowledge of travel and geography. *Match the city and its description.* Good luck!

A. Canton (China)
B. Choulou (Cyprus)
C. Inchon (Korea)

___ 1. Five hundred people live in my town. The land there is hilly and good for farming.

___ 2. It takes fifty minutes by train to go from my city to the capital. The principal product is salt.

___ 3. My city has a long history. It has many famous universities and buildings. It also has many, many food factories. In the spring, the ground is full of flowers. My city's other name is "flower city."

THE TANK WAS EMPTY
By John Lapatsanis

Six years ago I lived in Athens. Every fifteen days I went to my village with my friend who had a new Italian car. One Friday the engine didn't work. My friend got out of his car and looked at it. He didn't see anything. For one hour he and I looked everywhere. We checked everything. Finally, after one hour, we looked in the gas tank. It didn't have any gasoline! My friend and I felt terrible because the day before he had filled the tank, and today it didn't have any gasoline. Anyway, together we put gasoline in the tank and went to my village. In the end, my friend was lucky because the thief took only the gasoline. My friend still has his car.

MY DAUGHTER
By Gerardo Nuñez

I remember when my daughter was born. When I brought my wife to the hospital, I stayed there in the room with her. I put on doctor clothes and was able to see the birth of my daughter. She was beautiful. Then my wife and I were happy. Now my daughter goes to school in my country, and she practices gymnastics because she likes it. Also, all the time she draws with colors. She studies English and Spanish in her school, but I hope maybe for a short time she can go to study English in the USA. When my wife was a child, she lived in the USA for one year, and she spoke English very well. I hope that my daughter can study in the USA because she is very important to us.

WHY I LOOK ALMOST BALD
By Toru Imai

The reason that I shaved my head is not a heartwarming story. Yesterday I wanted to cut my hair. I didn't have a lot of money, so I looked for a cheap haircut. I found a salon with only $5.99 haircuts. I said to the barber, "My hair is so long." Then she shaved my side hair and made a favorite Chinese hairstyle in only three minutes! But, I'm Japanese. I said, "Shorter," and she said, "Oh, I see! You need to say Number 2!" She shaved my head all over in just one minute! She never thought or waited. It's the reason for the cheap price. I will never go for a cheap haircut again. Also, I learned that I need to study hairstyles in English *before* I go for a haircut.

NO MORE ACCIDENTS
By Ryota Imai

A few years ago, I got hit three times on my bicycle in two months. The first accident was at night in June. I was going across an intersection. A car hit my bicycle side, but the car was going slowly. The car driver said, "Are you okay?" I said, "I'm okay," but my right shin hurt. My bicycle was no problem. The second accident was at night in July. The car was a little fast, and I was thrown onto the hood of the car. The car driver said, "We are going to the hospital and the doctor can check you." My body was no problem, but my bicycle was broken. After three or four days, the car driver sent a new bicycle. The third accident was in the morning when I was going to school. That day I was feeling a little uneasy, and my uneasiness came true. I was hit by the side of a car, but we were going very slowly. The car driver and I exchanged addresses. After that, I went to school. My mother said, "If you get in another accident, you can die." I hope I don't have any more accidents.

6.3 Web sites

1 Discuss these questions with your class.

  1 Do you use the Internet? If so, how often and why?

  2 Which Web sites do you visit?

  3 Do you visit any Web sites written in English? If so, which ones and why?

2 With a partner or small group, answer the questions about the student Web site below.

Web Site Questions

1 What is the address of the Web site?

2 What information is in the banner at the top of the page?

3 What information is at the bottom of the page?

4 What is the name of the Web site?

5 Does the Web site give a date? If so, what is the date?

6 What kind of information do you expect to find on the Web site?

7 How many columns does the Web site have? What kind of information is in each column?

8 Is there a menu (table of contents, site map, index) of the Web site?

9 Does the Web site have links? Where do the links take you?

10 Is there advertising on the Web site? If so, where is it?

3 Work with a partner or small group. If you have access to the Internet, go to a Web site in English, and answer the questions in the box *Web Site Questions* on the opposite page.

6.4 Crossword puzzles

Crossword puzzles are a popular feature of newspapers and magazines. They are also easy to make, are fun to solve, and can provide valuable practice in answering and forming WH-questions.

A Solving a crossword puzzle

Work with a partner. Read the questions, and write your answers in the puzzle. (The answer key is on page 54.)

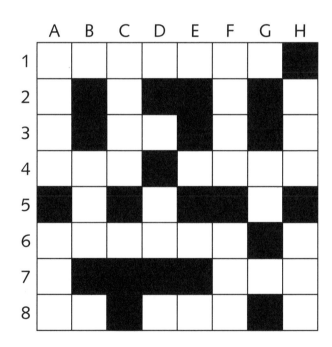

Across

1A   What language are you studying now?
3C   What is the opposite of *off*?
4A   What is a synonym of *unhappy*?
4E   What is another way to write OK?
6A   What is after *first*?
7F   How much is five minus four?
8A   What is the abbreviation of Texas?
8D   What does a chicken lay?

Down

A1   What is the opposite of *begins*?
A6   What is the past tense of *sit*?
B4   What is the plural of *is*?
C1   How do you feel when a friend sends you a long, interesting letter?
D5   What is missing? I always ___ my homework before I watch TV.
F1   How do you feel when your temperature is 102°F?
F6   What animal likes to chase cats?
G4   What is an abbreviation for morning?
H2   What is the fifth month?
H6   How many fingers do you have?

B Writing clues

1 Finish this crossword puzzle. Write one question for each word. You will write ten questions: four across and six down. Beside each question, you must write the number and letter (1A, D3, F5, etc.) that tell where to write the first letter of the answer.

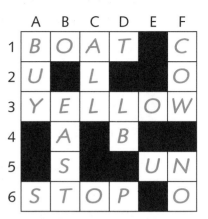

Across

1A *What do people use to travel on water?*

3A _____

_____

_____

Down

A1 _____

_____

_____

_____

_____

_____

2 Compare your questions with your classmates'. Decide who has written the best clues.

C Making a crossword puzzle

1 Make your own crossword puzzle by following these directions.

- Draw a grid of eight columns, labeled A–H, and eight rows, labeled 1–8.

- Put words in the grid, making sure that any two words touch in *only one* place. Write a question for each word. Blacken all the blank boxes.

- Make a clean copy of both the puzzle (without the answers) and the questions.

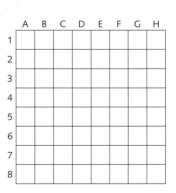

2 Exchange puzzles and questions with a classmate. Have fun!

3 You may wish to publish your crossword puzzles in a class publication. (See 6.6 on the next page.)

6.5 Independent-practice portfolio writing

1 Work with a partner or small group. Talk about the topics in the box.

2 Choose a topic from the box to write about in class or as homework. Focus on communicating your ideas. Do not worry about mistakes while you are writing, but be sure to reread and edit when you finish.

- Use good format and paragraph structure.
- Spend 15–30 minutes writing.
- Write 100–200 words.

> ### Topics
>
> Thinking about newspapers and Web sites
>
> *1* How does the Internet make your life better or worse?
> *2* Do you watch a great deal of TV news, do you avoid the news, or are you in between?
> *3* What is your favorite way of getting the news? Is it TV, Internet, radio, or newspaper?
>
> Looking inside and outside yourself
>
> *4* A pleasant memory
> *5* A problem in your community
> *6* A topic from the list on page 148

3 When you are finished, add your work to your portfolio.

6.6 A class publication

In this course, you and your classmates will publish some of your work to share with each other and other readers.

A Choosing a type of publication

1 Answer these questions with your class.

1 Which type or types of publications would you like to make?
2 What kinds of resources do you have? Computers? Copiers? Internet access?
3 What kinds of skills do you have in your group?

2 Choose the format you will use for the first publication: newspaper, magazine, Web site, or wall display.

B Planning the first publication

1 Choose one of your favorite pieces of work for the class publication from the writing that you have done so far.

- Personal experience stories from Unit 4
- Crossword puzzles from this unit
- Independent-practice portfolio writing

2 There are many different types of articles that are suitable for a class publication. Look at the sample student newspaper and Web site in this unit. Decide what you would like to include in your class publication.

3 Form committees to work on different parts of the class publication. Here are some examples.

- Editorial committee to collect and organize student writing
- Technology committee
- Photography committee
- Art and design committee
- Layout or paste-up committee, working on computer or on paper

Answer key for the puzzle
on page 51.

Part Two

Writing More, Writing Better

Unit 7 Follow These Steps

In this unit, you will describe how to do something. You will organize your composition by describing each step of a process.

7.1 Process dictation

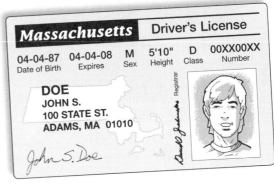

A Talking about getting a driver's license

1 Discuss these questions with a partner.

1 What process do these pictures show? How many steps are shown?

2 Do you have a driver's license? What information is on your driver's license?

3 When did you get your driver's license? What is the youngest age for drivers in your country or state?

2 Share your answers with the class.

B Dictation, Version 1

1 On a separate piece of paper, write the paragraph as your teacher dictates. Write the title in the center of the top line. Indent the first line of the paragraph. (The script for the teacher is in Appendix 2.)

2 Compare your paragraph to the one on the next page. Check punctuation, capitalization, spelling, and format. Circle any errors.

Steps in Getting a Driver's License

In the United States, teenagers can get a driver's license before becoming 18 by following three basic steps. First, they get a learner's permit by taking a course and a written exam on traffic laws. Next, they practice driving under adult supervision. Finally, they take a driving test for a regular license. Following this three-step process allows U.S. teenagers to drive at a young age.

(65 words)

C Talking about the dictation

1 Discuss these questions about the topic of the dictation.

　1 What is the difference between a regular license and a learner's permit?

　2 Who probably supervises teenagers learning to drive?

　3 According to the paragraph, what are the steps for getting a driver's license?

　4 How are these steps different from getting a license in another country? (You can use the Internet to investigate driving laws in different places.)

2 Discuss the structure of the dictation paragraph with the class.

　1 What is the topic of this paragraph?

　2 Underline the topic sentence in the paragraph.

　3 Underline the concluding sentence in the paragraph.

　4 What does the word *process* mean?

3 Read the file card below.

PROCESS

A process is a series of steps. Writers use signals to show the order of the steps. Chronology signals (time words) or enumeration signals (numbering words) can be used to show the steps.

The following sentences show two good ways to present steps in a process.

Chronology signals

First, teenagers take a course and a written test.
Next, they drive with a learner's permit.
Finally, they get a regular license.

Enumeration signals

The first step is taking a course and a written test.
The second step is driving with a learner's permit.
The third step is getting a regular license.

4 Circle the signal words in your dictation.

D Adding support

1 The ideas in this dictation paragraph need support. Talk with a partner to decide where to add this supporting information to the dictation paragraph.

   1 This step is very important in learning practical skills.

   2 Each state has a driver's handbook for learners to study.

   3 The hard part of this test is parallel parking.

   4 . . . usually with parents or older siblings.

2 Rewrite your dictation paragraph, adding the supporting details.

3 When you are finished, add your work to your portfolio.

E Self-correcting dictation

Cover the phrase or sentence below each line. Write on the line as your teacher dictates. Then, when your teacher says to check, uncover the words and check your writing.

1 _____

Steps in Getting a Driver's License

2 _____

By following a three-step process, U.S. teenagers can get a driver's license before becoming 18.

3 _____

First, they take a course and a written exam. Then, they get a learner's permit.

4 _____

The permit allows them to practice driving under the supervision of an adult.

5 _____

Finally, they must follow traffic laws during a driving test.

6 _____

Following three basic steps allows them to get a regular license at a young age.

F Dictation, Version 2

1 Study Dictation, Version 1 carefully to prepare for Dictation, Version 2, which is a variation of Version 1.

2 Write the Version 2 dictation paragraph as your teacher dictates. Give your paper to your teacher to check, or check your work as your teacher directs. (The script for the teacher is in Appendix 2.)

7.2 Revising process paragraphs

A Revising format and signal words

1 Read the first draft of the process paragraph below. Talk about it with a partner and then with your class. Decide where revisions are needed. If you need help revising this composition, review the *Format for a Student Paper* file card on page 20 and the *Process* file card on page 57.

> DRIVER'S LICENSE
>
> There are three easy step in getting a new driver's license. First step is studying the rules in the driver's handbook carefully. Next step is going to the driver's license office to take the written test. Final, is take the driving test. People who follow these two steps can get a driver's license easily.

2 Revise and rewrite the paragraph. Use either chronology signals (*first, next, finally*) or enumeration signals (*the first step, the second step, the third step*). Make all the necessary changes.

3 When you are finished, add your paper to your portfolio.

B Grouping steps in a process

1 Read Draft 1 of a composition below. With your class, answer these questions.

1 What is the topic of the paragraph?

2 What is the topic sentence of the paragraph?

3 How many steps are there in the process?

4 How many sentences are there about each step?

5 What is the concluding sentence of the paragraph?

6 What would be a good title for the paragraph?

> **Draft 1**
>
> A few years ago, my grandfather Paul, who loved to cook but did not like recipes, made an especially disgusting and memorable dish. It did not have a name, but here is his process. First, he looked in the refrigerator. Second, he got some leftover enchiladas. Third, he put the enchiladas in a saucepan. Fourth, he looked in the pantry. Fifth, he found two cans to add. They were a can of green beans and a can of hot dog chili sauce. Sixth, he added the green beans and hot dog chili sauce to the enchiladas. Seventh, he cooked the mixture on top of the stove until the food was very hot. This step took about fifteen minutes. Eighth, he put some crunchy dry cereal on top of the mixture. Finally, he served the dish in the saucepan. Unfortunately, as the pieces of cereal absorbed the liquid, they began to look like short, fat brown worms. This dish was unforgettable because it looked so disgusting that no one would eat it, except my grandfather.

2 Now read Draft 2 and answer the same questions as in B1. With a partner, discuss the differences between the drafts and decide which draft is better. Explain your reasons to the class.

Draft 2

A few years ago, my grandfather Paul, who loved to cook but did not like recipes, made an especially disgusting and memorable dish. It did not have a name, but here is his process. First, he looked in the refrigerator, got some leftover enchiladas, and put them in a saucepan. Then, he looked in the pantry and found two cans to add. They were a can of green beans and a can of hot dog chili sauce. Next, he cooked the mixture in a saucepan on top of the stove until the food was very hot. This step took about fifteen minutes. Finally, before serving the dish in the saucepan, he put some crunchy dry cereal on top of the mixture. Unfortunately, as the pieces of cereal absorbed the liquid, they began to look like short, fat brown worms. This dish was unforgettable because it looked so disgusting that no one would eat it, except my grandfather.

---

 3 Rewrite the paragraph below, grouping the seven steps into three. Add a good title.

Careful writers use a seven-step composing process to produce good work. First, they collect ideas. Second, they make a plan. Third, they write the first draft. These steps are usually easy when the topic is familiar or interesting. Fourth, they revise their work. The revising step requires making changes by adding, deleting, and reorganizing information. Fifth, they write a second draft that shows the changes. Sixth, writers must edit for mistakes. Finally, they share their work. Editing before sharing is important because most writers make small errors in spelling, grammar, and punctuation that need to be corrected. Some of these steps can take much longer than others do, and repeating steps is common. Following this seven-step process consistently can help improve anyone's writing.

7.3 Editing

A Editing practice

Rewrite these sentences correctly, using the editing symbols as a guide. (The editing symbols are explained in Appendix 4 on page 149.)

1 Careful writers *sv agr* wants to produce good work *p*

2 They follow these *#* step.

3 After sharing *ww* your *pro agr* work, they edit it carefully.

4 *art.* Composing process *wf* have seven *#* step.

5 *art.* First step *v* collecting ideas and writing *art.* first draft.

6 *○* Are seven steps in *art.* process composing.

7 Following this *sp* proces can improve *wf* me writing.

B Corrective format errors

Rewrite the paragraph below, correcting the formatting errors.

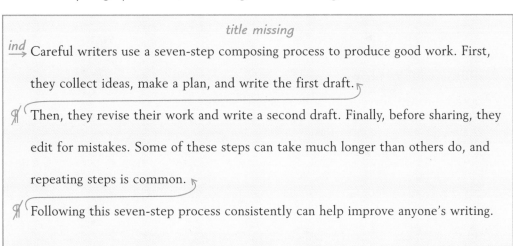

title missing

ind Careful writers use a seven-step composing process to produce good work. First, they collect ideas, make a plan, and write the first draft.

¶ Then, they revise their work and write a second draft. Finally, before sharing, they edit for mistakes. Some of these steps can take much longer than others do, and repeating steps is common.

¶ Following this seven-step process consistently can help improve anyone's writing.

7.4 Publication project: How-to Guide

A Brainstorming

1 What are you an "expert" on? What process can you explain? Tell the class one or two processes you can write about.

2 Work with a partner. Discuss the process topics below. Write other possible topics in the blanks. Then share your favorite topics with the class.

1 The process of studying for a vocabulary test

2 The process of planning a successful vacation trip

3 The process of giving a good oral presentation

4 The process of exploring for oil

5 _____

6 _____

7 _____

8 _____

B Outlining three basic steps

1 Choose a topic from the list in 7.4A on the previous page.

2 Tell your partner the process in just three basic steps. You partner will write down your topic and the three steps as you talk.

3 Listen to your partner and write down your partner's topic and the three steps.

Your partner's topic: _____

    A. _____

    B. _____

    C. _____

C Planning and writing

1 Choose a process to explain, and outline the three basics steps.

Your topic: _____

    A. _____

    B. _____

    C. _____

2 Write your paragraph. Use the dictation paragraph on page 57 as a model.

- Use formal style.
- Begin with a topic sentence about the process.
- Write about only *three* steps (not two steps, not four steps). You can group related steps together.
- Use chronology or enumeration signals to make the steps clear to the reader.
- Add a supporting sentence to explain each step.
- End with a concluding sentence that restates the ideas in the topic sentence.

D Publishing and sharing

1 After revising and editing your paragraph, make a *How-to Guide* for a class publication project. Use newspaper, magazine, booklet, Web site, or wall format. (See Unit 6 for more ideas about publishing.)

2 Read the collection of papers to learn something about each person's area of expertise. Ask and answer questions about each process.

3 Share your display or publication with other classes or other people.

7.5 Independent-practice portfolio writing

1 Work with a partner or small group. Talk about the topics in the box.

2 Choose a topic from the box to write about in class or as homework. Focus on communicating your ideas. Do not worry about mistakes while you are writing, but be sure to reread and edit when you finish.

- Use good format and paragraph structure.
- Spend 15–30 minutes writing.
- Write 100–200 words.

Topics

Thinking about driving

1 Steps in getting a driver's license in a specific country or state
2 Life without a car
3 A bad experience with driving
4 A funny incident while driving
5 The worst driver you know

Looking inside and outside yourself

6 Becoming independent
7 A local event, such as a concert, play, or festival
8 A topic from the list on page 148

---

3 When you are finished, add your work to your portfolio.

Unit 8 Class Statistics

In this unit, you will gather and organize simple statistics about your class and use them to write a paragraph.

8.1 Class data and statistics

Ages: 55   29   30   23   16   22   32   18   21   41

Data and statistics are important because writers often use them to support their ideas.

1 Look at the students in the Writing 310 English class and their ages. Answer the questions about them.

   1 What percentage of the class is male?

   2 What is the minimum age (youngest)?

   3 What is the maximum age (oldest)?

   4 What is their age range? From _____ to _____

   5 What is their average age? (To calculate the average, add all their ages and divide by the number of students in the class.)

2 In which school courses do you sometimes use data and statistics?

8.2 Math terms

These exercises will help you with basic math terms in English.

A Numbers

Listen to your teacher read the numbers. Fill in the missing numbers you hear. (The script for the teacher is in Appendix 2.) Then practice saying the numbers as the teacher directs.

1 1.5	5 ½	9 ¾
2 1.57	6 1½	10 ⁵⁄₄
3 _____	7 _____	11 _____
4 _____	8 _____	12 _____

B Math problems

1 Study how to write and say math problems. Practice reading the problems aloud with a partner or the class.

Addition	Subtraction
$3+2=5$ or $\begin{array}{r}3\\+2\\\hline5\end{array}$	$8-1=7$ or $\begin{array}{r}8\\-1\\\hline7\end{array}$
The **sum** of three and two **is** five. Three **plus** two **equals** five.	Eight **minus** one **equals** seven.

Multiplication	Division
$4\bullet25=100$ or $\begin{array}{r}25\\\times 4\\\hline100\end{array}$ or $4\times25=100$	$12\div2=6$ or $2\overline{)12}\,^{6}$
Four **times** twenty-five **equals** one hundred.	Twelve **divided by** two **equals** six. Two **into** twelve **equals** six.

2 Solve each problem, and then write it as a sentence.

1 $10+7=$ _17 Ten plus seven equals seventeen._

2 $4\bullet5=$ _____

3 $3\overline{)36}=$ _____

4 $11-2=$ _____

5 $50\div5=$ _____

6 $18,000\times1=$ _____

3 With the class, read each problem aloud, and say if it is addition, subtraction, multiplication, or division.

C Fractions and decimals

1 Study how to write and say these examples.

Fractions		
1 ½ = one-half	*or*	a half
2 5⅓ = five and one-third	*or*	five and a third
3 7¾ = seven and three-fourths	*or*	seven and three-quarters
Decimals		
1 0.87 = zero **point** eight seven	*or*	eighty-seven hundredths
2 3.01 = three **point** zero one	*or*	three and one hundredth
3 3.009 = three **point** zero zero nine	*or*	three and nine thousandths

2 Solve each problem. Then read the problems and answers aloud with your class.

1 $1.5 + 2.25 =$ _____

2 $2.5 - 1.3 =$ _____

3 $0.5 \times 0.3 =$ _____

4 $½ + ¼ =$ _____

5 $2 - ⅔ =$ _____

6 $5 ÷ ½ =$ _____

D Percents

1 Study how to write and say these examples. Practice reading the examples aloud with a partner or the class.

1 100% = one hundred **percent** (*or* **a** hundred percent)	
2 50% = fifty **percent**	50% of 12 = 6
3 25% = twenty-five **percent**	25% of 200 = 50
4 33.3% = thirty-three **point** three **percent**	33.3% = ⅓
5 16.7% = sixteen **point** seven **percent**	16.7% = ⅙
6 87.5% = eighty-seven **point** five **percent**	87.5% = ⅞

2 Solve each problem.

1 ³⁄₆ = ½_____ = 50_____ %

Example: *Three sixths equals one half. One half is equivalent to fifty percent.*

2 ⁵⁄₉ = _____%

3 ⁹⁄₁₀ = _____%

4 ¾ = _____%

5 10% of 25 = _____

6 50% of 25 = _____

3 Check your answers with the class. Explain how you got your answer.

E Tables, ranges, and averages

1 Answer the questions about Table 1 with your class.

   1 What is the name of this table?

   2 How many columns are there?

   3 How many rows are there?

   4 How many types of bags are there?

   5 How many types of information about each bag are in the table?

   6 What do the abbreviations mean?

Table 1
Types of book bags used by various class members

Class members and their bags				
Name	Tom		John	
Type of bag		Tote bag		Backpack
Dimensions W x H x D	18" x 10" x 8"	_____ x 11" x 6"	17" x 12" x _____	13" x _____ x 4"
Weight	_____ lbs.	2 lbs.	2¼ lbs.	_____ lb.
Cost	$15.00	$16.99		$27.00

W = width H = height D = depth x = by " = inches lb(s). = pound(s)	

2 Listen to your teacher and fill in the blanks in the table. (The script for the teacher is in Appendix 2.)

3 With a partner, ask and answer questions about the minimum and maximum *width, height, depth, weight,* and *price* of the bags in the table.

   Example: A: What is the minimum depth?
   B: 3 ½ inches

4 Complete these sentences.

   1 The bags range in _____ from 1 to 2¼ pounds

   2 The bags _____ in width from _____ to 18 inches

   3 The bags range in _____ from 10 inches to 17 inches.

   4 The bags _____ in price from _____ to _____.

   5 The bags range _____ depth _____ 3½ inches _____ 8 inches.

5 Calculate the following averages with a partner. Explain each step that you take to reach your answer.

1 Average width: _____

2 Average height: _____

3 Average depth: _____

4 Average weight: _____

5 Average price: _____

6 Use a ruler showing feet and inches to measure the width, height, and depth of three or four student book bags in your class. Talk about the ranges and averages.

8.3 Organizing data into a paragraph

The students in the Writing 310 class, shown in 8.1, did a survey to collect data about their class in order to write a paragraph for their Web site. In the following activities, you will use their survey data to practice writing a paragraph using statistics as support.

A Demographic vocabulary

1 Take turns reading the sentences aloud with a partner. For each sentence, choose the correct heading from the box, and write it in the blank.

age	marital status	size of hometown
length of time here	native languages	countries and continents
living situation	occupations	number and gender of students

_____ 1 These students come from cities and towns that range in size from 1,000 to four million people.

_____ 2 Sixty percent of the students are married, and forty percent are single.

_____ 3 In their countries, they had a variety of occupations. For example, four were students, one was a mechanic, and another was a doctor.

_____ 4 They speak the following native languages: Japanese, Spanish, Russian, French, and Swahili.

_____ 5 The students range in age from 16 to 55 years. Their average age is 28.7.

_____ 6 They come from six countries in Africa, Asia, North America, and Europe.

_____ 7 The class consists of ten students; half are males, and half are females.

_____ 8 The students have been here for varying lengths of time. One student has been here for two years, and another student has been here for only one week. The average length of time here is 5½ months.

_____ 9 Three students live alone, and one student lives with a roommate. The other sixty percent live either with their spouses and/or with relatives.

2 Compare your answers with the class.

B Organizing information

1 Read the file card below.

GROUPING INFORMATION

In a paragraph, it is important to group related information together to create a logical order. Grouping information is very important because it helps readers understand ideas more easily.

The sentences about the students in the Writing 310 class, for example, could be grouped for a paragraph in the following way:
• All the sentences about *home country* together.
• All the sentences about *situation now* together.

2 Work with a partner. Answer these questions about how to organize the sentences in 8.3A into a paragraph.

1 Which sentences are about *home countries*? What is the best order for those sentences in a paragraph?

2 Which sentences are about the *situation now*? What is the best order for those sentences in a paragraph?

3 In the paragraph, would you place the sentences about *home countries* before the sentences about *situation now*? Why or why not?

C Using generalizations in a paragraph

Paragraphs that present data often begin and end with sentences that make accurate general statements, or generalizations, about the data.

1 Which generalization is the better topic sentence for a paragraph of the sentences from 8.3A? Why?

1 The students in the Writing 310 class in the English Program have many things in common.

2 The Writing 310 class in the English Program is varied and interesting.

2 Which generalization is the better concluding sentence for the paragraph? Why?

1 All in all, the Writing 310 class is very diverse and fascinating.

2 All in all, the people in the Writing 310 class are remarkably similar and homogeneous.

D Writing a paragraph

1 Write a paragraph with the sentences from 8.3A and the better sentences from 8.3C, grouping the sentences in logical order. Add the title, "Meet Writing 310."

2 When you are finished, add it to your portfolio.

8.4 Revising and editing

A Revising to group information

1 Read the paragraph below with your class. The order of the sentences needs improvement. Answer the questions.

1 What is the main idea about California?

2 Which are the topic sentence and the concluding sentence?

3 What are the four types of data in the paragraph? Group the sentences for each type.

4 What is the logical order for the sentences to make a good paragraph?

California in 2000

(1)Among the many ethnic groups in California, the largest groups are whites (59.5%), Hispanics (32.4%), Asians (10.9%), and blacks (6.7%). (2)This makes it the most populous state in the United States. (3)About a quarter of the population is under the age of 18. (4)Few visitors to California know many statistics about the state. (5)The population has grown 13.6% since 1990. (6)Just over half of the population is female. (7)The smallest reported group is Native Hawaiian and Other Pacific Islanders (0.3%). (8)Visitors who are interested in more statistics about California can find them at http://quickfacts. census.gov/gfd/states. (9)One tenth is 65 years or older. (10)According to the 2000 U.S. Census, California has a population of more than 33,871,000.

---

2 Rewrite the paragraph.

3 When you are finished, add it to your portfolio.

B Editing practice

Rewrite these sentences, using the editing symbols as a guide. (The editing symbols are explained in Appendix 4 on page 149.)

1 These students come four diffrents continents.

2 Forty percents of the students married, and 60 percent single

3 Ten students, three woman and seven mens, are in this english class.

4 This class has a̲ economist, a civil engineer, a lawyer, a computer scientst and six students
   wf   *sp*
   whom are working on them degree.
   wf   *wf*   *#*

5 The students ranges in age from 20 to 33 years, and average age is 26.5.
              sv agr   *art.*

8.5 Composition

In this section, you and your classmates will prepare a table for collecting data about your class. Then, you will work together to collect and analyze the data and write a composition about your class.

A Making a table to collect data

1 On a piece of paper, make a table for in-class data collection. Copy the example below, adding enough rows for five students.

1. Name	2. Living situation	3. Languages	4.	5.	6.	7.	8.	9.
What's your name?	Who do you live with?	What languages do you speak?						
1.								
2.								

2 Work with your class. From the list below, choose six more headings for the table. Write them in columns 4–9 of your table.

Occupation	Continent	Years studying English
Country	Length of time here	Marital status
Name and size of hometown	Age	Reason for learning English

3 With your class, decide on a good question to ask for each of the six headings that you chose. Then write the questions into the second row of your table

4 Work in a small group of no more than five students. Take turns asking each other the questions. Fill in the information in the table. Use the Internet to find hometown population information, if necessary.

B Compiling data

Work with members of other groups. Combine their data with yours and complete the *Data Summary Sheet* with data about all the students in the class. If you have no data for a particular category, write n/a, which stands for "not applicable."

Data Summary Sheet

1. Number of people in class: _____   Percent Male: _____   Percent Female: _____

2. Living situation: Alone: _____   With a family member: _____   With a roommate: _____

3. Languages: Number of different languages: _____

List them: _____

4. Occupations: Number of full-time students: _____

List other occupations: _____

5. Countries: Number of different countries: _____

List them: _____

6. Continents: Number of different continents: _____

List them: _____

7. Hometown: Largest: _____   Population: _____

Smallest: _____   Population: _____

8. Length of time here: Maximum: _____   Minimum: _____   Average: _____

9. Age: Maximum: _____   Minimum: _____   Average: _____

10. Years studying English: Maximum: _____   Minimum: _____   Average: _____

11. Marital status: Married: _____   Single: _____

Divorced: _____   Separated: _____

Widowed: _____

12. Reasons for learning English: Number of different reasons: _____

List the two most common: _____

C Writing about your class

1 Write a paragraph about your class, using the statistics from the *Data Summary Sheet* in 8.5B. Revise and edit very carefully, reporting all the data accurately.

2 Publish the paragraph in the class newspaper or on the class Web site, or share it with others in another way.

8.6 Independent-practice portfolio writing

1 Work with a partner or small group. Talk about the topics in the box.

2 Choose a topic from the box to write about in class or as homework. Focus on communicating your ideas. Do not worry about mistakes while you are writing, but be sure to reread and edit when you finish.

• Use good format and paragraph structure.

• Spend 15–30 minutes writing.

• Write 100–200 words.

Topics

Thinking about your class

1 Your opinion about the best kind of English class (Big or small? Same or different ages? Same or different native languages?)

2 Interesting things you have learned from or about your classmates

3 A funny story about something that happened in your class

Looking inside and outside yourself

4 Two important days in your life

5 The weather in your country

6 A topic from the list on page 148

---

3 When you are finished, add your work to your portfolio.

Unit 9 The Perfect Routine

In this unit, you will write paragraphs about daily routines, practice adding sensory details, and form complex sentences.

9.1 Ms. Lee's daily routine

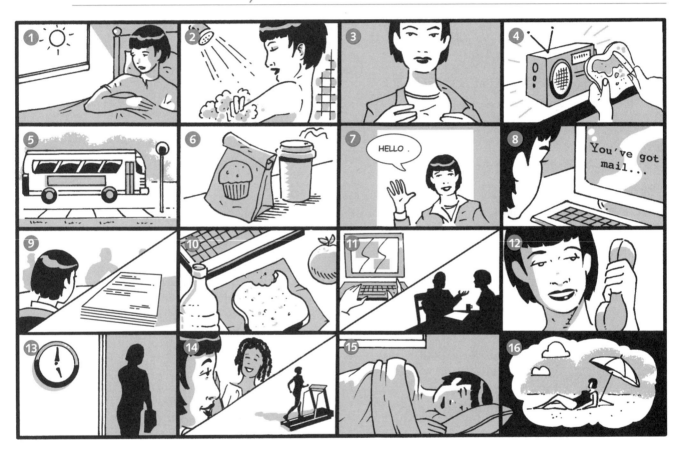

A Learning vocabulary

1 Liz Lee is a single woman who works for a computer software company. During the week, she follows a daily routine to help her manage her busy life. Listen to your teacher read about Ms. Lee's daily routine. What is your opinion of her routine? Is it healthy, boring, or stressful? Discuss with your class. (The script for the teacher is in Appendix 2.)

2 Listen again to sentences about her routine. They are not in the same order as the pictures. As you listen, fill in the blank with the matching picture number. (The script for the teacher is in Appendix 2.)

A ____   B ____   C ____   D ____   E ____

F ____   G ____   H ____   I ____   J ____

K ____   L ____   M ____   N ____   O ____   P ____

B Completing sentences

Fill in the blanks in these sentences. Each sentence corresponds to the picture in 9.1A with the same number.

1 Liz _____ up.

2 She _____ a _____.

3 She gets _____.

4 She listens _____ the news while she _____ her lunch.

5 She _____ the bus _____ work.

6 She _____ at a _____ to pick _____ coffee and
a _____.

7 She _____ to the office and _____ hello.

8 She _____ her e-mail.

9 She _____ paperwork and goes to _____.

10 She _____ lunch at her _____.

11 She _____ at her computer and _____ clients.

12 She _____ telephone calls.

13 She gets _____ work.

14 She gets _____ with friends or works _____ at the gym.

15 She goes _____ bed.

16 She dreams _____ the _____ and her _____ vacation.

9.2 Complex sentences

A Practicing complex sentences with *before* and *after*

Work with a partner. Practice asking and answering questions about Liz's routine. Use the examples and the framework below to help you form the questions and answers.

What does Liz do | before / after | she _____ ?

Q: What does Liz do *before* she gets dressed?
A: Before she gets dressed, she takes a shower.

Q: What does Liz do *after* she checks her e-mail?
A: After she checks her e-mail, she does paperwork and goes to meetings.

B Writing complex sentences

1 The sentences you formed in 9.2A are called complex sentences. They have two clauses. Read the file card below.

COMPLEX SENTENCES

A complex sentence has two parts:
- a main clause (S + V)
- a subordinate clause (S + V)

Subordinate clauses begin with a signal word, such as *before, after, while, when, because,* and *although.*

    S   V   S   V
Joe has breakfast *before* he gets dressed. (no comma)
    main clause   subordinate clause

    S   V   S V
Joe reads the newspaper *because* he is interested in current events. (no comma)
    main clause   subordinate clause

       S   V   S V
While Joe rides the bus to work, he reads the newspaper. (comma required)
     subordinate clause   main clause

        S   V   S V
Although Joe eats breakfast, he is hungry by 9 A.M. (comma required)
    subordinate clause   main clause

2 Mark the subject and verb in both clauses in these sentences. Then underline the subordinate clauses. The first one is completed for you. (See Mini-Handbook pages 137–8 for more on complex sentences and how to punctuate them.)

           S   V   S   V
1 After Liz gets up, she takes a shower.

2 She makes her lunch because she wants to save money.

3 While she makes her lunch, she listens to the news.

4 When she gets off the bus, she stops at a stand to pick up coffee.

5 Before Liz has her lunch, she does paperwork.

6 Liz's daily routine is very helpful although it is often boring.

3 Two of the sentences above do not have commas. How are these two sentences different from the others? Rewrite the sentences, using commas.

4 Complete these complex sentences by adding a main clause. Use a comma when necessary.

1 After Liz gets dressed, *she makes her lunch* _____.

2 _____ before she gets to the office.

3 _____ after she says hello.

4 Although Liz uses a computer at work, _____ .

5 Because Liz works out at the gym, _____ .

6 _____ before she goes to bed.

7 While she sleeps, she _____ .

C Writing a paragraph

1 Write a paragraph. Form complex sentences with the sentences from 9.1B. Add the sentences and phrases below.

1 Liz's weekday routine is often monotonous, but it helps her deal with her busy life.

2 Liz Lee is a busy person with a useful daily routine.

3 Liz's Weekday Routine

4 at 5 P.M.

5 at 5:30 P.M.

6 about 10 P.M.

2 When you are finished, add your work to your portfolio.

9.3 Editing sentence structure

A Three common mistakes

1 Read the file card about three common mistakes that students often make with sentence structure.

> ## FRAGMENTS, RUN-ONS, AND COMMA SPLICES
>
> Here are three common sentence mistakes.
>
> **Fragment** → *frag*
> The writer uses a subordinate clause as a complete sentence.
>
>   *frag*
>   She takes the bus. Because it is very convenient.
>   She takes the bus because it is very convenient.
>
> **Run-on** → *RO*
> The writer puts two main clauses together without a subordinator.
>
>   *RO*
>   She gets up early she takes an important exam.
>   She gets up early before she takes an important exam.
>
> **Comma splice** → *CS*
> The writer puts two main clauses together with a comma instead of end punctuation.
>
>   *CS*
>   Every day is the same, she has the same routine.
>   Every day is the same. She has the same routine.

2 Correct these sentences. Each one has a common mistake in sentence structure.

1 She picks up a snack she gets to the office.
^{RO}

_____

2 Her job is busy, she likes it.
^{CS}

_____

3 After she works out at the gym. She goes to bed early.
^{frag}

_____

4 Her daily routine is boring, she wants to change it.
^{CS}

_____

5 She leaves work at 5 P.M. Because she wants time to work out.
^{frag}

_____

B Editing practice

1 Rewrite the paragraph below, using the editing symbols as a guide. (The editing symbols are explained in Appendix 4 on page 149.)

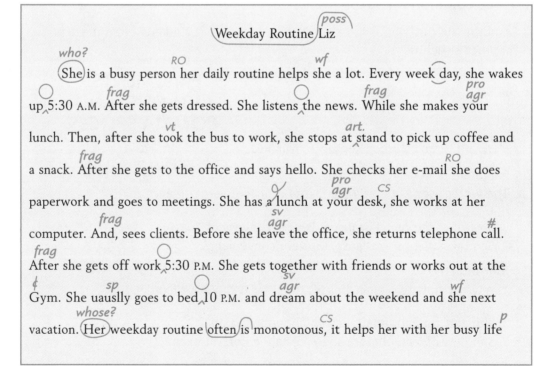

2 When you are finished, add it to your portfolio.

9.4 Composition: A routine day

A Interviewing your partner

1 Work with a partner. Take turns interviewing each other. Partner A closes the book. Partner B asks the questions below and takes notes of Partner A's answers. Then change roles.

> ### Interview Questions
>
> 1 When do you wake up? Do you get up immediately?
> 2 What do you do before you go to school or work?
> 3 When do you leave home?
> 4 How do you get to work or school? What do you do on the way? How long does it take you?
> 5 When does your work or school start? Are you always on time?
> 6 What do you do at work or school? When do you take breaks?
> 7 When do you get off work or get out of school? When do you leave?
> 8 Do you go directly home? If not, what do you do?
> 9 How do you get home?
> 10 When do you get home?
> 11 What do you do as soon as you get home? Do you always do the same thing?
> 12 When do you eat? Do you cook? How often do you eat out?
> 13 What do you do in the evening? Do you always do the same thing?
> 14 When do you go to bed? Do you go to sleep at once?
> 15 How long do you sleep? Do you remember your dreams?

2 What's your opinion about your partner's routine? Write three opinion adjectives. You will use one or more of these adjectives later in your topic sentence and your concluding sentence.

_____   _____   _____

B Writing about your partner's routine

1 Write a paragraph about your partner's routine day, using your notes from 9.3A.

- Use a title.
  Example: *Li Ming's Routine Day*

- Begin with a topic sentence that includes your opinion of your partner's routine. You can use one or more of the opinion adjectives you wrote in 9.4A2.
  Example: *My classmate Li Ming has a very unusual routine day.*

- Use time signals to show the chronological order of events. Look at the *Chronology* file card on page 80 for examples.

- Use compound and complex sentences to combine events.

- Write a concluding sentence that repeats the opinion adjective(s) in your topic sentence.

- Use a computer if possible so you can easily revise and edit in later activities.

CHRONOLOGY

Chronology or chronological order is a good organizational pattern for telling the time order of events. Chronological order is useful in writing stories, biographies, and historical accounts.

Here are some signals that show time order.

Yesterday she got up *at 5:30* A.M.

In 1967, he moved to Canada *after* he finished college.

In the mornings, he goes jogging *before* going to work.

2 Give your first draft to your partner to read. Ask him or her to tell you if the information is correct and complete.

3 Make any necessary changes your partner suggests.

C Revising by adding information

1 Reread and analyze your composition. Look at your notes or talk to your partner for additional information.

1 How many "before school" actions did you include? _____
   Write a complex sentence with *after* that tells about two more actions.

   _____

2 How many "at school" actions did you include? _____
   Write a complex sentence with *while* that tells about two more actions.

   _____

3 How many "at home" actions did you include? _____
   Write a complex sentence with *when* that tells about two more actions.

   _____

4 How many "in the evening" actions did you include? _____
   Write a complex sentence with *before* that tells about two more actions.

   _____

 2 Write the second draft of your composition. Add your new sentences in appropriate places.

D Editing feedback

1 Check your composition. In the column marked *Your answers*, answer each question with *Yes* or *No*.

Editing Checklist	Your answers	Partner's answers
1 Are the person's name and the writer's opinion used in both the topic and concluding sentences?		
2 Does each sentence begin with a capital letter and end with a period?		
3 Are all the verbs in the simple present tense?		
4 Are chronology signals used in the paragraph?		
5 Are all the pronouns (*he/him/his* or *she/her/her*) used correctly?		
6 Are there at least four complex sentences with *before, after, when,* or *while*?		
7 Do these complex sentences have a subject and a verb in both the main clause and the subordinate clause?		

2 Exchange compositions and books with a partner. In the column marked *Partner's answers*, answer each question with *Yes* or *No*. Do not make any corrections on your partner's composition.

3 Compare how you and your partner answered the questions about your compositions. Discuss how you can each improve your compositions.

E Writing the final draft

1 Write the final draft. Make any necessary changes that you discussed with your partner in D3.

2 Publish your final draft in the class newspaper or on the class Web site, or share it with others in another way.

A Talking about perfect routines

1 Read the following newspaper advice column. Answer this question with your class: What does Dr. Noe Itall want his readers to do and why?

PSYCHOLOGY CORNER

Fast Way to a New Life

Doctor Noe Itall

Are you tired of your daily routine? Are you bored with your typical days? You *can* change your life. Here is the important first step.

Use your imagination! Imagine that you *now* have your perfect routine. You wake up at the perfect time, and you eat the perfect breakfast. You put on the perfect clothes. Perhaps you have the perfect job and go to work the perfect way. You have *exactly* the schedule that you like best. Imagine your perfect days *in detail* and write to me about this routine. Begin your letter like this: "Dear Dr. Itall: I now have the perfect routine for me. Every morning, I . . ."

When you finish your letter, send it to me. I will read it. Maybe I will print it here in my column, so keep reading "Psychology Corner."

---

2 Tell your classmates some things that you do *not* like about your present routine.

B Imagining a perfect routine

Use your humor and imagination to create your own perfect routine.

* Maybe you go to work by helicopter.
* Maybe you travel by horse.
* Maybe a hair stylist visits you every morning.
* Perhaps you feed your pet alligator every afternoon.

Spend a few minutes filling in the chart on the next page with your ideas. Do *not* write sentences; write only words and phrases. Work quickly. Write as many ideas as you can. Be wild and crazy! Have fun!

In the morning	
In the afternoon	
In the evening	

C Adding sensory details

Sensory details are very important in writing vivid descriptions. They tell about what you *see, hear, smell, feel,* and *taste* and make your description "come alive" for your readers, giving them the feeling of "being there" with you.

1 Read the file card below.

SENSORY DETAILS

Sensory details make writing vivid. In your writing, they will help readers understand your ideas.

When writing, try to include all five senses.

See The morning sky is full of white fluffy clouds.

Hear The birds outside my bedroom window sing cheerfully.

Taste I love the clean taste of tea when I wake up.

Smell When I meet my friend, her perfume makes me smile.

Feel When we cross the river, the wind blows my hair.

2 Write the name of the appropriate sense in each blank.

1 _____ a dead animal under the house

2 _____ the soft night air on my face

3 _____ a pink helicopter with silver trim

4 _____ the wind in the trees

5 _____ ice cream on a hot day

3 Look at your notes about a perfect routine in 9.5B. Spend a few minutes adding sensory details to your activities. Use all five senses.

D Writing a letter

1 Write a letter about your perfect routine to Dr. Noe Itall.

- Review correct letter format in the *Features of a Letter* file card on page 5.
- Use the ideas and sensory details in your notes in 9.5B.
- Use humor and imagination. Try to make your readers smile and laugh.
- Begin your letter:

  Dear Dr. Noe Itall:
  Now I have a perfect routine. Every morning I . . .

- Conclude your letter:

  This is the perfect routine for me because . . .

2 Reread and revise your perfect routine letter, making sure that it has interesting sensory details.

3 Reread and edit your letter, making sure that you have no fragments, comma splices, or run-on sentences.

4 Write a final draft of your letter. Then decide with your class how to share the letters.

9.6 Independent-practice portfolio writing

1 Work with a partner or small group. Talk about the topics in the box.

2 Choose a topic from the box to write about in class or as homework. Focus on communicating your ideas. Do not worry about mistakes while you are writing, but be sure to reread and edit when you finish.

- Use good format and paragraph structure.
- Spend 15–30 minutes writing.
- Write 100–200 words.

> **Topics**
>
> Thinking about routines
> 1 Your own daily routine
> 2 Your routine on the weekend
> 3 A new routine that could improve your life
>
> Looking inside and outside yourself
> 4 Your earliest memory
> 5 Tips for shopping
> 6 A topic from the list on page 148

3 When you are finished, add your work to your portfolio.

Unit 10 Great Trips

In this unit, you and your classmates will take a trip and write about it. There are two trips to consider – a virtual online trip and an actual field trip. You will also do a class activity during the trip.

10.1 A virtual trip

Great Virtual Trips!

1 The Metropolitan Museum of Art in New York, New York, www.metmuseum.org. Visit the collections and click on "Director's Choices," which shows twenty-five of the director's favorite objects.

2 California Academy of Sciences in San Francisco, California, www.calacademy.org. It offers nice online tours of exhibits in the natural history museum and aquarium.

3 The White House in Washington, D.C., www.whitehouse.gov/history/whtour. You can take a room-by-room tour of the presidential residence.

4 The Natural History Museum in London, England, www.nhm.ac.uk/museum/vr/index.html. There is a tour of the online gallery of virtual objects. You can grab and rotate the objects.

5 The Museum of Modern Art in New York, New York, www.moma.org/collection/collection_highlights.html. You can choose a collection and see the highlights of one or more galleries.

6 National Baseball Hall of Fame in Cooperstown, New York, www.baseballhalloffame.org/help/tour.htm. You can see baseball artifacts and read about baseball history.

7 National Gallery of Australia, Canberra, www.nga.gov.au. It provides an interesting virtual tour of an Aboriginal art exhibit and other exhibits.

8 The University of Texas in Austin, Texas, www.utexas.edu/tower/. Visit the main building of the university to see both the inside rooms and the view of the university from the top of the tower.

A Planning a virtual trip

1 With your partner or group, discuss the Web sites in the list above, and talk about which ones seem interesting.

2 Choose three of the Web sites to visit (or visit Web sites suggested by your teacher).

B Taking a virtual trip

1 Read the questions below before you take your virtual trip.

Virtual Trip Questions

1 When did you take the virtual trip?

2 Who took the virtual trip with you?

3 Web site 1:
   a Where is this place actually located?
   b What did you see on this Web site?
   c What was your opinion of this Web site?

4 Web site 2:
   a Where is this place actually located?
   b What did you see on this Web site?
   c What was your opinion of this Web site?

5 Web site 3:
   a Where is this place actually located?
   b What did you see on this Web site?
   c What was your opinion of this Web site?

6 How many minutes did the virtual tours take?

7 What did you like best?

8 Did you have any trouble during the tours?

9 Which Web site do you think other people might like?

2 With your partner or group, visit the three Web sites you chose in 10.1A. Spend about ten minutes at each site. Enjoy looking around, but remember to take some notes. Speak English together during the trip!

3 With your partner, write answers to the questions.

C Reporting about the virtual trip

1 With your partner(s), give a brief oral report about your trip to the class.

2 Write a paragraph about your trip.

* Use your notes and the answers you wrote to the *Virtual Trip Questions*.

* Begin with a topic sentence that gives basic information and your opinion about the virtual trip.

* Write sentences about each of three Web sites, using chronological order signals to present the Web sites in order. (Review the *Process* file card on page 57 and the *Chronology* file card on page 80.)

* End with a concluding sentence that restates the opinion in the topic sentence.

3 Share your paragraphs about the trip by displaying them in your classroom. Publish the best paragraph(s) in the class publication or on your class Web site.

10.2 A real trip

A Choosing a place of interest

1 With your class, brainstorm some interesting places for a real class trip. Write the names of the places below.

- Museum: _____
- Exhibit: _____
- Zoo: _____
- Park: _____
- Interesting neighborhood: _____
- Tourist attraction: _____
- Other places of interest: _____

_____

_____

_____

2 Choose a place for your trip.

B Planning and collecting information

1 Discuss these points with your class, and make as many decisions as possible. If you cannot make the trip as a whole class, go with a partner or a small group, and discuss the points below with the person(s) who will accompany you.

- Date of the trip _____
- Time of departure and return _____
- Costs (transportation, admission ticket, meal, or snack) _____
- Place to meet _____
- Type of transportation _____
- Place to eat _____
- Clothing _____
- Things to take (camera, umbrella, sports equipment, food, notebook)

_____

2 Decide what information or research is still needed to plan the trip. Decide who will get what information. You may need to make a telephone call or visit a Web site.

C A trip activity

1 Do this activity during your trip.

1 During the visit, choose a mystery object, such as a painting at a museum or an animal at the zoo.

2 Write a description, or draw a picture of the mystery object in the top half of a piece of paper. In the bottom half of the paper, write the name of the mystery object.

2 After your trip, do this activity in your classroom.

1 In the classroom, divide into two teams.

2 Tear your trip activity paper in half, separating the descriptions and answers.

3 Put all of your team's descriptions together, and separately put all of the answers together.

4 Give the two groups of papers to the other team. The other team will give you its descriptions and answers.

5 Each team tries to match the descriptions and drawings to the answers.

6 The winner is the first team to identify all the mystery objects.

Activity Form

Write a description, or draw a picture of the mystery object here.

Write the name of the mystery object and, if available, other important information, such as the artist's name.

D Class trip composition

1 The questions below will help you gather information for your class trip composition. The questions are not in any special order. Change the questions to fit your situation.

Class Trip Questions

1 How many people went on the trip?

2 What was your opinion of the trip?

3 What did you do while you were there?

4 Tell about your lunch or snack. (Where did you eat? What did you eat?)

5 What was the place like? Describe it.

6 When did you go home?

7 How did you get home?

8 When did you arrive at the place?

9 How did you get there?

10 Who met the group at the place? When? Where?

11 What did you like best?

12 What happened after you ate?

13 When did you meet at school? When did you leave school?

14 What day and date did you go?

2 With your class, take turns answering the questions, using complete sentences. When the class has agreed on an answer, a student "secretary" can write it on the board (or on a transparency or big sheet of paper).

3 When all the questions are answered, edit your answers together with your teacher.

4 On your own, write a paragraph about the class trip that includes all the answers. Follow these steps.

- Begin with a topic sentence giving an opinion about the trip.
- Write the body of your paragraph using chronological order signals to present the events in order. (Review the *Process* file card on page 57 and the *Chronology* file card on page 80.) Organize your sentences by grouping related supporting details about each part of the trip.
- End with a concluding sentence that restates the opinion in the topic sentence.

E Revising

1 As a class, read two or three class trip paragraphs chosen by your teacher. Look for good chronological and logical order.

2 Discuss the organization of the sentences in each paragraph. Decide which paragraph has the best organization, and explain why. If any further revision or editing is needed, work with the class to make the changes.

F Publishing and sharing

1 Put the best paragraph(s) in your class publication or on your class Web site, along with any photographs that you had taken during the trip.

2 Turn your paragraph into a cloze exercise (for an example of a cloze exercise, see the newspaper article entitled "Level Two at Met and Park" on page 48.) Give your cloze exercise to a classmate to do.

10.3 Independent-practice portfolio writing

1 Work with a partner or small group. Talk about the topics in the box.

2 Choose a topic from the box to write about in class or as homework. Focus on communicating your ideas. Do not worry about mistakes while you are writing, but be sure to reread and edit when you finish.

- Use good format and paragraph structure.
- Spend 15–30 minutes writing.
- Write 100–200 words.

Topics

Thinking about trips

1 A trip that you want to take someday

2 Your favorite vacation

3 Your favorite Web site related to traveling

Looking inside and outside yourself

4 How you feel about working out

5 Why kids like dinosaurs

6 A topic from the list on page 148

3 When you are finished, add your work to your portfolio.

4 Choose one of your independent-practice portfolio assignments to revise and edit for sharing in your class publication project.

Unit 11 Info Expo

> In this unit, you will focus on classification and write a paragraph that classifies something into three main types. To share your information, you will organize an *Info Expo.*

11.1 Classification dictation

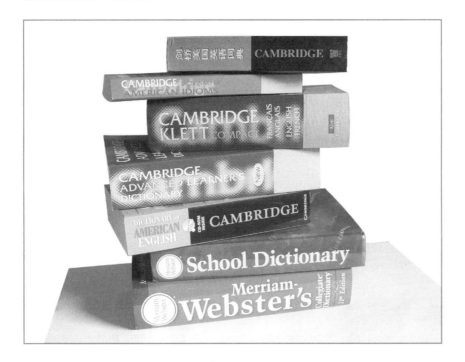

A Talking about dictionaries

1 Discuss these questions with your partner.

1 What types of dictionaries are in the photo?

2 What types of dictionaries do you have at home? At school?

3 What other types of dictionaries can you think of?

4 What type of dictionary do you prefer to use when you are studying English?

2 Share your answers with the class.

B Dictation, Version 1

1 On a separate piece of paper, write the paragraph as your teacher dictates. (The script for the teacher is in Appendix 2.)

2 Compare your paragraph with the one on the next page. Check punctuation, capitalization, spelling, and format. Circle any errors.

Advice about Dictionaries

People studying English usually want a dictionary. There are three main types to consider. One main type is a bilingual dictionary. Another main type is a dictionary for learners of English. Still another main type is a dictionary for native speakers of English. Therefore, before buying, students should think carefully about which of these three main types is best for them.

(61 words)

C Talking about the dictation

1 Discuss these questions about the topic of the dictation.

1 What kinds of information does a dictionary contain?

2 What do these words mean: *consider, dictionary, bilingual*? Look up each of them in your dictionary to check the meaning and part of speech.

3 What are the advantages and disadvantages of a bilingual dictionary?

4 Which type of English dictionary is best for you right now? Why? How about in the past? In the future?

2 Discuss the structure of the dictation paragraph with your class.

1 What is the topic of the dictation paragraph?

2 What is the concluding sentence in the paragraph?

3 What type of organization is used in this paragraph?

3 Read the file card below, and answer the questions that follow.

CLASSIFICATION

Classification divides things into types or parts. Enumeration signals make it clear to the reader when discussion of one type ends and discussion of a new type begins. (See the *Enumeration Signals* file card on page 102 to see three common sets of signal words and phrases.)

Examples of topic sentences of classification paragraphs

There are three main types of _____ to consider.

_____ can be divided into three main types.

People have three main types of _____ to choose from.

Examples of sentences with enumeration signals

One important type of _____ is . . .

Another basic category of _____ is . . .

Still another common kind of _____ is . . .

1 What is classified in the dictation paragraph?

2 How many main types are mentioned in this paragraph? What are they? Circle the enumeration words that signal these types.

3 Which word (or words) shows the opinion of the writer?

D Adding support

1 The ideas in the dictation paragraph need support. Talk with a partner to decide where to add this supporting information to the dictation paragraph.

  1 For example, it tells whether a noun is count or noncount.

  2 It includes old forms of words and historical information about them, so it is sometimes difficult to understand.

  3 It has easy definitions and special information, such as example sentences and usage notes, for people learning English.

  4 . . . because each type serves a different purpose . . .

  5 It translates words from English into another language, and vice versa.

  6 . . . good . . .

2 Rewrite the dictation paragraph, adding the supporting details.

 3 When you are finished, add your work to your portfolio.

E Self-correcting dictation

 Cover the phrase or sentence below each line. Write on the line as your teacher dictates. Then, when your teacher says to check, uncover the words, and check your writing.

1 _____

Advice about Dictionaries

2 _____

Before buying a dictionary, learners should consider three main types.

3 _____

Students of English should buy the best type of dictionary for them.

4 _____

Still another type to think about is a dictionary for learners of English.

5 _____

People wanting a dictionary should think carefully before buying one.

F Dictation, Version 2

1 Study Dictation, Version 1 carefully to prepare for Dictation, Version 2, which is a variation of Version 1.

 2 Write the Version 2 dictation paragraph as your teacher dictates. Give your paper to your teacher to check, or check your work as your teacher directs. (The script for the teacher is in Appendix 2.)

11.2 Reading and outlining

1 Read the paragraph carefully. As you read, think about what is classified and how many types are enumerated. Circle the enumeration signals.

Popular Types of Student Housing

When U.S. students leave home and move to another city to attend a university, they have three popular types of housing to consider. One popular type is student dormitories. Dorms are especially good during the first year because they usually provide meals and offer opportunities for making friends. Another popular type of housing is apartments. They are especially good for people who like to cook or have special dietary or personal needs. Still another popular type of housing is student cooperative houses, sometimes called co-ops for short, which are available near many American universities. In these democratically-run houses, students do household tasks, such as cooking, shopping, or cleaning, to keep the operating costs low. Thus, before signing a contract, students should think carefully about the best type of housing for them.

---

2 Use the lines below to make an outline of the paragraph.

Topic: _____

    A. _____

    B. _____

    C. _____

11.3 Revising and editing

A Adding supporting details

1 Computers can be classified into three main types: desktops, laptops, and servers. With a partner, discuss the differences among these three types of computers.

2 The paragraph in the box below is short and well organized, but it needs additional supporting details. Rewrite the paragraph, and add three sentences: one about the laptop computer, one about the desktop computer, and one about the server.

3 When you are finished, add your work to your portfolio.

Types of Computers in the Workplace

These days almost every company has computers, which can be divided into three basic types, according to their function. One basic type of computer is the laptop computer. It is small and portable. Another basic type is the desktop computer. It is the most common type because it is economical to buy. Still another basic type of computer is the server for the local network. Today, the server is not large in physical size, but it has a lot of computation power and memory. These three basic types are used in companies everywhere.

(99 words)

B Editing practice

1 Read and edit the paragraph in the box below.

- Use the editing symbols to make corrections where needed. (The editing symbols are explained in Appendix 4 on page 149.)
- Refer to the *Format for a Student Paper* file card on page 20 and the *Classification* file card on page 92.
- Check your corrections with a partner and the class.

> Common types of web sites ⟶ *center title*
>
> Web sites can be divided into three common types one common type is a personal
>
> site. Individual use these type of site for to share photos with friends. Other
>
> common type of website is a commercial site, businesses can use it to sell or
>
> advertise products and services.
>
> Still other common type is an informational site. Universities, government
>
> agencies, and organization use these type to provide informations to the
>
> public.
>
> Most of people use all three type of web sites.

2 Rewrite the paragraph, making all necessary corrections.

3 When you are finished, add your work to your portfolio.

11.4 Publication project: Info Expo

A Talking about expositions and fairs

1 Look at the photos on the next page, and answer the questions with a partner and then the class.

1 Where are the students? What are they doing?

2 What does the name *Info Expo* mean?

3 The theme of this *Info Expo* is the environment. What topics are these students talking about?

2 Discuss expositions or fairs you have attended or know about.

1 What did you do or see there?

2 Why do people attend expositions and fairs?

B Planning and brainstorming for *Info Expo*

1 Work with your class to plan an *Info Expo.*

1 What will be the theme of your *Info Expo*? Here are some ideas:

- Your school or campus
- Your city, state, or country
- People, things, or events
- Your profession or a job

2 Who will you invite to come?

- Other people at your school
- Family and friends
- Others

2 Look at these examples of *Info Expos* planned by other students.

Audience	Other people at this school
Theme	Environmental problems in the world
Possible topics	Types of environmental problems Important categories of waste material Three kinds of pollution

Audience	Our class
Theme	Information about our countries
Possible topics	Principal types of industries in Mexico Popular kinds of tourist attractions in Korea Categories of music in Brazil

3 Work with a partner. Decide on an audience and a theme. Then brainstorm some possible topics for your *Info Expo.* Write ideas in the blanks below.

Audience	
Theme	
Possible topics	

4 Share your ideas with the class.

C Planning and writing the first draft

1 Choose your topic, and write your outline here.

Topic: _____

    A. _____

    B. _____

    C. _____

2 Write the first draft of your paragraph. Use the dictation and the paragraphs in this unit as your guide. Follow these guidelines.

- Use formal style.
- Begin with a topic sentence about the three types of something.
- Use an adjective in the topic sentence to give your opinion.
- Write about three types only (not two types or four types, just three types).
- Use enumeration signals to make your organization clear to the reader.
- Add sentences with supporting details to explain each type.
- End with a concluding sentence that restates the main idea.

D Publishing and sharing

After revising and editing your paragraph, publish this information in one of the following ways:

- Hold an *Info Expo.* Make a poster to illustrate the three types of things in your paragraph. Make copies of your paragraph to give to visitors. Help arrange a display of posters in your classroom. Invite people to view the display.
- Make a booklet, a special newspaper section or edition, or a Web link for the class publication project. Share your publication with other readers.

11.5 Independent-practice portfolio writing

1 Work with a partner or small group. Talk about the topics in the box.

2 Choose a topic from the box to write about in class or as homework. Focus on communicating your ideas. Do not worry about mistakes while you are writing, but be sure to reread and edit when you finish.

- Use good format and paragraph structure.
- Spend 15–30 minutes writing.
- Write 100–200 words.

> **Topics**
>
> Thinking about expositions
> 1 An exposition you attended
> 2 An event or display you helped organize
> 3 An exposition or fair in your local area now
>
> Looking inside and outside yourself
> 4 Your name and how you feel about it
> 5 An English-language video or movie in your local area now
> 6 A topic from the list on page 148

3 When you are finished, add your work to your portfolio.

Unit 12 Exercise Opinions

In this unit, you will focus on exercise and sports topics. You will combine sentences, do dictations, and write paragraphs that list reasons or facts to support your opinion.

12.1 Getting some exercise

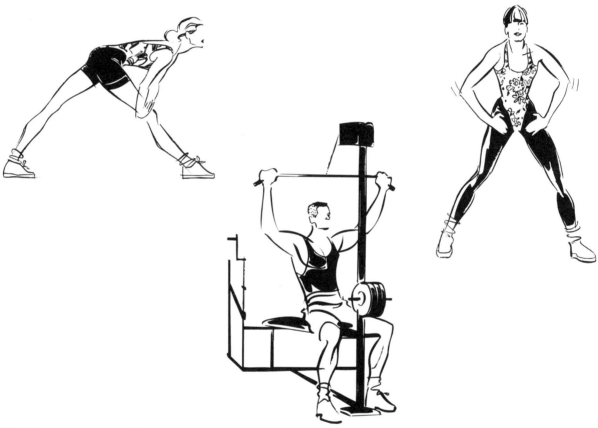

1 Discuss exercise with your class.

　1 Which of the three types of exercise in the illustrations do you prefer: stretching, aerobic exercise, or working out with weights? Why?

　2 What kind of exercise do you usually do?

　3 Why do you exercise? Do you usually get enough exercise?

2 Do a stretching activity with your class. Follow your teacher's instructions. (The script for the teacher is in Appendix 2.) When you have finished, answer these questions:

　1 Was the exercise fun?

　2 How do you feel now? Better or worse?

3 Look at the diagram below. Read the recommendations in the "Ergonomic Workstation Checklist" for how to sit at a computer. Read them aloud with your class to practice the vocabulary.

ERGONOMIC WORKSTATION CHECKLIST

Sources: *Cornell University Ergonomics Program, Occupational Safety and Health Administration*

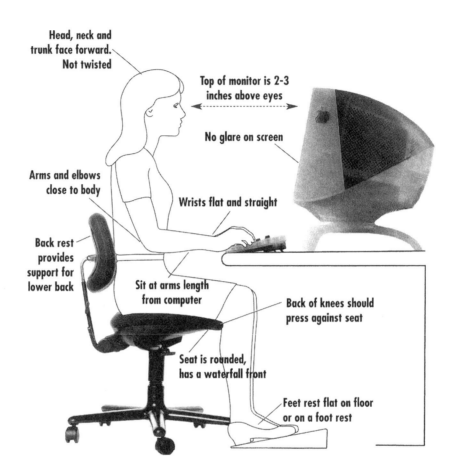

Head, neck and trunk face forward. Not twisted

Top of monitor is 2-3 inches above eyes

No glare on screen

Arms and elbows close to body

Wrists flat and straight

Back rest provides support for lower back

Sit at arms length from computer

Back of knees should press against seat

Seat is rounded, has a waterfall front

Feet rest flat on floor or on a foot rest

4 Discuss these questions with your class.

1 What does *ergonomic* mean?

2 Do you get a neck ache, headache, or backache when working at the computer? Do your wrists get sore?

3 What exercises can help you avoid these problems?

4 How can you improve your posture at a desk or computer?

12.2 Sentence combining

A Getting ready

1 Write three questions as your teacher dictates them. (The script for the teacher is in Appendix 2.)

2 As the teacher reads the paragraph in Appendix 2, listen for the answers to the questions you wrote. Then, answer them with the class.

3 Write three more questions as your teacher dictates them.

4 As your teacher reads the paragraph again, listen for answers to the questions you wrote. Then, answer them with the class.

B Combining sentences orally

Work with the class. Orally combine each pair of sentences into one longer sentence. Use each of these words at least once: *and, but, so, although, because*. Say the sentences only. Do not write or take notes.

1 a Exercise is important for everyone.
  b Not everyone gets enough.

2 a More and more people have sedentary jobs.
  b They rarely use their large muscles.

3 a These workers sometimes get exercise on sunny weekends.
  b They need easy ways to get exercise every day.

4 a They can learn some easy ways from these three people.
  b They can have healthier lives.

5 a The first person, a very important lawyer, has a nice car.
  b She walks to work every day.

6 a She wears an elegant suit under her coat.
  b She has old jogging shoes on her feet.

7 a She carries her dressy shoes in her briefcase.
  b She wants to keep them clean.

8 a The second person, a successful accountant, drives her car to work.
  b She adds physical activity to her daily routine in a different way.

9 a She parks her car very far from her office building.
  b She takes the stairs instead of the elevator.

10 a She also walks with co-workers during lunch.
  b She often stands up while making phone calls.

11 a The third person, a computer programmer, exercises his eyes every hour.
  b He wants to avoid eyestrain and headaches.

12 a He also stands up and stretches beside his ergonomic computer workstation.
  b He wants to prevent back pain.

13 a Exercise is important to these three busy people.
  b They find ways to get enough.

C Writing a paragraph with longer sentences

1 Write each pair of sentences in 12.2B as one sentence. Write the new sentences as a paragraph, indenting the first line.

2 When you are finished, add your work to your portfolio.

12.3 Dictation: Why people exercise

A Dictation, Version 1

1 On a separate piece of paper, write the paragraph as your teacher dictates. (The script for the teacher is in Appendix 2.)

2 Compare your paragraph with the one on the next page. Check punctuation, capitalization, spelling, and format. Circle any errors.

B Talking about the dictation

1 Discuss these questions about the topic of the dictation.

 1 What are the three reasons why people exercise?

 2 Which sentences express facts and which express an opinion?

 3 The *cardiovascular* system has two parts. What is the "cardio" part? What is the "vascular" part?

 4 Which food has more calories?

  a A potato or a tomato?

  b A salad or a pizza?

  c A cup of milk or a cup of black coffee?

2 Discuss the organization of the dictation paragraph with your class.

 1 What is the topic sentence in the paragraph? Underline it. Does it express an opinion?

 2 What type of organization is used to develop this paragraph?

 3 What is being enumerated (numbered or listed) in this paragraph? Draw a box around the word that tells the thing enumerated.

3 Read the file card.

ENUMERATION SIGNALS

There are several sets of useful enumeration signals.
- All sets of signals are good.
- Choose the set that works best with your topic.
- Don't shift back and forth among sets.

Here are three sets of enumeration signals:

Set A	Set B	Set C
Some people	*One* reason	*The first* reason
Other people	*Another* reason	*The second* reason
Still others	*Still another* reason	*The third* reason

---

4 Which set of enumeration signals is used in the dictation paragraph? Find and circle the enumeration signals in the paragraph.

> **Dictation, Version 1**
>
> Why People Exercise
>
> Why do people exercise? Some people exercise for their cardiovascular health. Other people exercise for their appearance. They try to burn more calories because they want to lose weight and look better. Still other people exercise for fun and relaxation. In fact, most people probably exercise for all three reasons.
>
> (50 words)

C Adding support

1 The ideas in the dictation paragraph need support. Talk with a partner to decide where to add this supporting information to the dictation paragraph.

   1 . . . and build firm muscles . . .

   2 They enjoy themselves when they exercise.

   3 They want to build strong hearts and circulation.

   4 People exercise for many different reasons.

 2 Rewrite the paragraph, adding the additional sentences and phrases.

 3 When you are finished, add your work to your portfolio.

D Self-correcting dictation

 Cover the phrase or sentence below each line. Write on the line as your teacher dictates it. Then, when your teacher says to check, uncover the words and check your writing.

1 _____

Why People Exercise

2 _____

Why do people exercise?

3 _____

Most people exercise for reasons of relaxation, appearance, and health.

4 _____

Because some people want to lose weight, they try to burn more calories.

5 _____

Some people exercise for fun, and others exercise for cardiovascular health.

6 _____

In fact, most people probably try to exercise for all three reasons.

E Dictation, Version 2

1 Study Dictation, Version 1 carefully to prepare for Dictation, Version 2, which is a variation of Version 1.

2 Write Version 2 of the dictation paragraph as your teacher dictates. Give your paper to your teacher to check, or check your work as your teacher directs. (The script for the teacher is in Appendix 2.)

12.4 Reading about reasons

When expressing an opinion, writers give reasons to support their opinion. Each reason needs to be supported by details and examples.

1 Read the paragraph below and discuss these questions with your class.

  1 What is the topic of the paragraph?

  2 Is the main purpose of this paragraph to state facts or to express an opinion?

  3 How many reasons does the writer give?

Why Football Is Successful on U.S. Television

Football is a very successful sport on U.S. television for several reasons. One reason is that football has lots of action. Viewers do not get bored while watching football because something happens on every play. In a sense, each team wins, loses, or ties on every play, so viewers stay interested. Another reason for football's TV success is that viewers can actually see the game better on TV than in person. Close-up camera shots, multiple cameras, and instant replay make the sofa at home as good as the best seat in the stadium. Still another reason for football's success on TV in the United States is that it is good for advertising. Because there are frequent short breaks in the game, advertisers have many opportunities to show commercials to large audiences without interrupting the action. In short, because football pleases both TV viewers and advertisers, it is a big success on U.S. television.

---

2 Outline the paragraph by filling in the blanks below.

Topic: _____

  A. _____

  B. _____

  C. _____

12.5 Revising and editing

A Revising practice

1 With the class, discuss how to rewrite the paragraph you wrote in 12.3C if the second sentence of the paragraph is changed to the one below. Talk about a new title, a new first sentence, and changes to the enumeration signals and grammar that you will need to make.

New second sentence: *The first reason is to improve cardiovascular health.*

 2 Rewrite the paragraph as you discussed.

 3 When you are finished, add your work to your portfolio.

B Editing practice

1 Read the paragraph. With a partner, discuss the editing symbols and the changes that are needed.

 2 Rewrite the composition making all necessary changes.

> Reasons for Going to a Gym
>
> Different people go to a gym for different reason. # ww One people go to a gym for ww to work out with weights. Another people go to a gym for to take exercise classes in # aerobics or yoga. Other still go to a gym, because they can meet new people and ww make friends outside work. There are anothers reasons for going to a gym, these are cs three important ones.

 3 When you are finished, add your work to your portfolio.

12.6 Fact and opinion

A Talking about facts versus opinions

1 Talk with your class about the difference between a fact and an opinion.

2 Read the sentences in the box, and circle words that signal an opinion. Label the columns as *Facts* and *Opinions.* Compare your answers with a partner and then your class.

A _____	B _____
All sports are boring.	Some people exercise to lose weight.
Everyone should exercise.	Soccer is popular in many countries.
Jogging is the best exercise.	Not everyone gets enough exercise.

③ Read each sentence, and mark it with an *F* for fact or *O* for opinion.

1 _____ People should exercise thirty minutes every day.

2 _____ Exercise is important for everyone.

3 _____ Football is popular in the United States.

4 _____ It is hard for most office workers to get exercise on the job.

5 _____ Computer jobs are usually sedentary.

6 _____ People must join a gym to get enough exercise.

B Giving opinions

Answer these questions with your class. Give reasons for your opinion.

1 Do you feel better or worse after you exercise? Why?

2 In general, do you think that exercise is good? Why or why not?

3 Do you think sports in general are good? Why or why not?

4 Is it easy to get enough exercise every day? Why or why not?

12.7 Opinion publication

A Getting ready to write

① Read the invitation in the box. Find the expressions *opinion poll* and *readers speak out*. Discuss their meaning with the class.

② Read the questions in the invitation in the box aloud, and discuss them with the class.

In Every Issue:	In-Depth Opinion Poll
FOCUS ON SPORTS & EXERCISE	**Readers Speak Out**

TELL US WHAT YOU THINK!

Every publication wants to hear from its readers. We are eager to know what you think and why you think so. We like to publish your opinions so that you can read and react to each other's ideas. Lately, we've been getting a lot of e-mail with questions and concerns from readers, so we'd like you to SPEAK OUT on the following topics:

Should Physical Education Be Mandatory in Schools?
What Is the Best Team Sport?
Does TV Have Too Many Sports Programs?
Is Hunting a Good Sport?
What Is the Best Type of Exercise for Losing Weight?

In 100–200 words, write your opinion on one of these topics, giving three reasons. Send us your work, and then read the next issue to find out what everyone is thinking.

And, THANK YOU FOR TELLING US YOUR OPINION!

B Brainstorming reasons

1 Form a discussion circle of three to six students who want to discuss the same question in the box in 12.7A.

2 In your discussion circle, brainstorm opinions and reasons. Each person gives an opinion and a reason, as in the following example.

Topic: Is bowling a bad sport?

Student A: Bowling is a bad sport because bowlers don't get fresh air.
Student B: Bowling's bad because you can easily hurt your wrist.
Student C: Bowling's good because you can do it no matter what the weather.

As you brainstorm, list each person's opinion and reason below.

Topic: _____

   A. _____

   B. _____

   C. _____

   D. _____

   E. _____

   F. _____

3 Read the opinions and reasons you wrote above. Choose the opinion you want to write about, and circle the three reasons that you think best support it.

C Writing, revising, and editing

1 Write the first draft of an opinion paragraph. Follow these guidelines.

- Begin with a topic sentence that includes your opinion.
- Write about three reasons (just three reasons and no more).
- Use enumeration signals to make your reasons clear to the reader.
- Add sentences with supporting details to make each reason clear and interesting.
- End with a concluding sentence that restates the topic and your opinion about it.

2 Revise and edit your opinion paragraph.

D Publishing your work

1 Make a feature for a class publication project called "Your Turn – Readers Speak Out." Display the opinion pieces in a newspaper, magazine, Web site, or in your classroom.

2 Read your classmates' paragraphs. Then discuss similarities and differences in the opinions and reasons. What are some of the more popular opinions or reasons?

12.8 Independent-practice portfolio writing

1 Work with a partner or small group. Talk about the topics in the box.

2 Choose a topic from the box to write about in class or as homework. Focus on communicating your ideas. Do not worry about mistakes while you are writing, but be sure to reread and edit when you finish.

- Use good format and paragraph structure.
- Spend 15–30 minutes writing.
- Write 100–200 words.

Topics

Thinking about sports and exercise

1 A question from the list on page 106 that your group did not discuss
2 A good/bad experience with sports or exercise
3 A great time at a sports event
4 A great sports event, such as a championship game

Looking inside and outside yourself

5 A member of your family you especially love
6 A holiday you enjoy
7 A beautiful outdoor spot
8 A topic from the list on page 148

---

3 When you are finished, add your work to your portfolio.

Unit 13 Portraits of Special People

In this unit, you will write a paragraph about a special person, focusing on three good qualities of this person and using examples as support. You will display your paragraphs in a class portrait gallery.

13.1 Portraits

A Talking about portraits

1 Museums, public buildings, universities, and some businesses have portrait galleries. Here visitors can see a collection of paintings or photographs of people. Discuss these questions with your class.

   1 What are portraits?

   2 What is a gallery?

   3 Where have you seen portraits?

2 Discuss these questions with a partner and then the class.

   1 What types of people are seen in portraits?

   2 Why do artists and photographers make portraits?

   3 Why do people like to look at portraits?

B Choosing people for a class portrait gallery

1. Just as artists draw portraits, writers can make portraits too. With a partner, brainstorm about special people to put in the class portrait gallery. These can be friends, favorite family members, teachers, or famous people.

2. Write the names of special people and their relationship to you. For example, *Professor Bell, my piano teacher.*

Person	Relationship to me
_____	_____
_____	_____
_____	_____
_____	_____

3. Choose a person to write about for the class portrait gallery. Then describe this person to your partner.

C Reading a portrait of a special person

1. Read this portrait of a grandmother. It focuses on the grandmother's personal qualities.

> ### My Grandmother
>
> Elizabeth (Lizzie) Wood, my grandmother, died many years ago, but she is still one of my favorite people. Although she was too strict, she had many good qualities. One of these was her love of learning. She had little money and lived on a farm, but she wanted to learn as much as possible. For example, after she finished all eight grades at her rural school, she took a one-month course in teacher training. It was the maximum education available to her. When she was old, she often took out her world globe after dinner and studied the countries on it. Another of Lizzie's good qualities was her ability to cook everything well. Without written recipes, she made delicious bread and desserts, such as fruit pies. She turned ordinary potatoes into tasty soup and ordinary apples into wonderful jelly. Still another of her good qualities was that she was helpful to everyone. One time she organized a drama production for kids in her community. Another time she was the president of a service organization. Many times she helped her neighbors with the hard parts of their sewing. Grandma Wood was a strict person, but her good qualities made her one of my favorite people.

2 Answer these questions with a partner, and check your answers with the class.

　　1　What does the word *quality* mean?

　　2　Which qualities does the writer mention?

3 Reread the paragraph, and circle the enumeration signals the writer uses to introduce each of the three good qualities.

13.2 Personal qualities

Thomas Alva Edison was a famous U.S. inventor. Two of his inventions were the electric light bulb and the motion picture camera.

A Stating qualities

The words below describe Edison's qualities. Label each word noun (*n*) or adjective (*adj*). Then write sentences stating Edison's good qualities.

1　a　creative　　　　*adj*　　One good quality was that he was creative.

　　b　creativity　　　*n*　　　One good quality was his creativity.

2　a　curiosity　　　_____

　　b　curious　　　　_____

3　a　determination　_____

　　b　determined　　_____

4　a　energetic　　　_____

　　b　energy　　　　_____

5　a　self-confidence　_____

　　b　self-confident　_____

B Giving examples

1 Read the file card below.

EXAMPLES

To signal an example, use one of the phrases in italics.

For example, she never forgets my birthday.

For instance, he plays piano at a community center.

One time, I called her at midnight to ask a question.

Another time, she loaned me some money.

Many times, he volunteered to help me with a big project.

He makes beautiful wooden gifts, *such as* pens and jewelry boxes.

---

2 With a partner, discuss which qualities each sentence in the file card illustrates. For example, if a person never forgets a birthday, the quality might be a good memory or thoughtfulness.

3 Reread the paragraph "My Grandmother" in 13.1C. Find an example of each of her three good qualities. Underline the words used to signal the examples.

C Matching qualities with supporting examples

1 Match each quality with an example about Edison.

Qualities	Examples
_____ 1 He was energetic.	a Edison asked questions constantly.
_____ 2 He was creative.	b He worked on things that people wanted. He tried to make things that did not break easily, that were easy to fix, and that worked in ordinary conditions.
_____ 3 He was a good organizer.	c He organized the first industrial research lab. There he directed teams of people in systematic research.
_____ 4 He had intense curiosity.	d He often did thousands of experiments to perfect an invention. For example, he did over 10,000 experiments to make a cheap battery for cars.
_____ 5 He had great determination.	e He went to school for only three months.
_____ 6 He was self-educated.	f Edison always worked very hard and seldom slept more than four hours a day.
_____ 7 He was practical.	g He made over 1,000 inventions during his lifetime.

2 Check your answers with a partner, by reading aloud and adding an example signal from the file card.

Example:
He was energetic. For instance, he always worked very hard and seldom slept more than four hours a day.

13.3 Portrait composition

A Planning your paragraph

1 With your teacher and class, brainstorm a list of qualities.

2 For each quality that you list, think of some examples of what people do that illustrate that quality.

3 Think about the person you chose to write about in 13.1B. Make a list of three good qualities of that person. Give an example of what that person does to show that quality.

Qualities	Examples of the qualities
_____	_____
_____	_____
_____	_____

B Organizing your paragraph

1 Organize your paragraph by completing the sentence outline below. Write two examples of each quality.

Topic: Three good qualities of _____

   A. One good quality is his/her _____

      1. For example, he/she _____

      2. _____

   B. Another good quality is _____

      1. _____

      2. One time, _____

   C. Still another good quality is _____

      1. For instance, _____

      2. _____

2 Explain your outline to a partner. As you talk, use signals for enumeration and for examples to make the three good qualities and the examples clear to your partner.

C Writing the paragraph

1 Review and revise your outline in 13.3B, and make improvements or changes if needed.

2 Write the first draft of your paragraph. Use signals for enumeration and for examples.

D Revising

1 Read this paragraph an American student wrote about his best friend. Follow these steps.

1 Underline the topic sentence. Find the three qualities of the person, and circle the enumeration signals for each one.

2 Draw a line through irrelevant sentences, and add appropriate words to signal the examples.

3 Compare your ideas with a partner. Check your answers with the class.

A Great Friend

Kyle Robertson, my best friend from childhood, has three good qualities that I admire. His sister's name is Emily. The first quality is his energy and sense of adventure. We visited his grandparents in Georgia. His grandfather drives a Volvo. We went to see my uncle in San Francisco. We went skiing, backpacking, or rock climbing together. A second quality is his technical skills. In junior high, we spent hours at the computer as "pilots" of simulated planes and, in high school, flew remote-controlled planes. Now we enjoy different activities. We like building Web sites and editing videos together. A third good quality is that he is loyal. He is always there for me, no matter when or where. I recently needed last-minute help at 4 A.M. with an important Java assignment. I love computers. There was no problem when I telephoned and woke him up, and he had an answer to my question, as always. In short, Kyle has many good qualities and is really a special friend.

---

2 Revise your own paragraph. Follow these steps.

1 Underline the topic sentence.

2 Find the three qualities of this person, and circle the enumeration signals.

3 Find the examples of these qualities. Underline words used to signal examples. If some examples need signals, add words in appropriate places.

4 Make any other changes necessary, and write the second draft.

E Editing

1 Cover the editing symbols while you read the following portrait of a special person. Mark the mistakes while you read. There is one mistake per sentence. (The editing symbols are explained in Appendix 4 on page 149.)

2 Uncover the editing symbols, and compare your answers with the symbols.

		Rick Porter, my close friend and neighbor for many years, has
#	ⓥ	many good quality. One good quality his delightful sense of humor.
sv agr		For example, he always have a new joke to tell at parties. Even if he
art.		makes a mistake when he is telling joke, he can still make everyone
ww		laugh. Other good quality is that he is interested in new things. For
sv agr.		example, if he hears a new song that he likes on the radio, he call and
		asks the disc jockey for the name of the CD and details about the
		artist. One time, when he heard about a new type of Honda, he
vt		investigated it on the Internet, contacted a local dealer, and takes a
		test-drive as soon as the new models arrived. Still another good
wf	pro agr	quality is his open-minded friendly. She likes to meet new people, on
		the beach, in the gym, or at a friend's dinner party, and finds the best
ⓢ		in everyone. People like him because is tolerant of people's lifestyles,
		interested in their hobbies, ready to talk about any topic, and rarely
#		critical of anything. This three good qualities make Rick a special
		person and wonderful friend.

3 Discuss with your class the mistakes and how to make corrections.

4 Rewrite the composition, making all necessary changes. When you are finished, add your work to your portfolio.

5 Edit the second draft of your own paragraph, which you wrote in 13.3D. Following your teacher's editing symbols, make sure your final copy is ready to be included in the class portrait gallery.

13.4 Publication project: Portrait gallery of special people

1 To share your compositions about special people, use the format of the class newspaper, magazine, Web site, or wall display to make a gallery of people who are special to your class.

2 Write one question about the special person in your portrait for your classmates to answer while reading.

3 Enjoy the portraits by reading them and answering the questions written by the writers.

13.5 Independent-practice portfolio writing

1 Work with a partner or small group. Talk about the topics in the box.

2 Choose a topic from the box to write about in class or as homework. Focus on communicating your ideas. Do not worry about mistakes while you are writing, but be sure to reread and edit when you finish.

- Use good format and paragraph structure.
- Spend 15–30 minutes writing.
- Write 100–200 words.

Topics

Thinking about special people and portrait galleries
1 Why you chose the person you did for the gallery
2 Portrait of another special person
3 A trip to a local museum or art gallery
4 A special pet

Looking inside and outside yourself
5 Successes and/or problems you had with the portrait assignment
6 Your favorite composition so far in the course
7 Advice for travelers
8 A topic from the list on page 148

---

3 When you are finished, add your work to your portfolio.

Unit 14 An Armchair Visit

In this unit, you will write a paragraph and learn how to expand it to an essay. Your essay will be part of a team project to take readers on "an armchair visit" to an interesting geographic area.

14.1 Dictation: The proud state of Texas

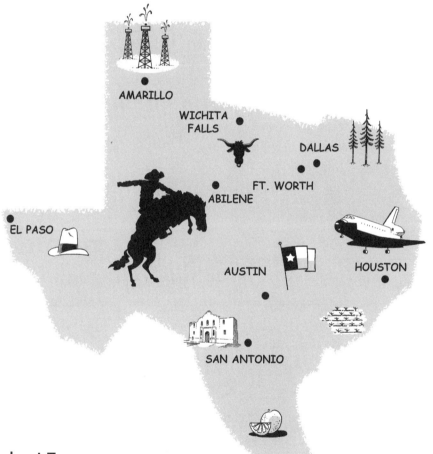

A Talking about Texas

1 Look at the map for one minute. Close the book, and draw a map of Texas on your own paper. Then, compare your map with this one.

2 Discuss these questions with your class.

1 What part of the United States is Texas in?

2 What country does Texas border?

3 Look at the map of Texas. Where in Texas can each of these things be found?
   a Oil wells   d Pine forests
   b Rice fields   e Oranges and grapefruit
   c Cattle ranches   f Space research

4 What else do you know about Texas?

B Dictation, Version 1

1. On a separate piece of paper, write the paragraph as your teacher dictates. (The script for the teacher is in Appendix 2.)

2. Now compare your paragraph with the one on the next page. Check your punctuation, capitalization, and spelling. Circle any errors.

C Talking about the dictation

1. Discuss these questions about the topic of the dictation with a partner.

   1. What is Texas famous for? Name four things.
   2. How long does it take to drive across Texas?
   3. Which word means *unhappy*?
   4. Why were Texans upset when Alaska became the forty-ninth state?
   5. According to Texans, what was Alaska made of?

2. Discuss the structure of the dictation paragraph with your class.

   1. What is the topic of this paragraph?
   2. Where is the topic sentence?
   3. What is the key word in the topic sentence? What other vocabulary words in the paragraph are related to this key word?
   4. Is there a concluding sentence in this paragraph?

3. Read the file card below.

ANECDOTES

An anecdote is a brief story that a writer puts in a paragraph or an essay.

An anecdote usually has one of these purposes:
- To support an idea in a paragraph.
- To introduce the topic and get the reader's attention.

4. Discuss these questions with a partner.

   1. What is the anecdote in the dictation paragraph?
   2. Is it used to support an idea or to introduce the topic?

Dictation, Version 1

The Proud State of Texas

Texas is known around the world for its oil wells, cattle ranches, and cowboys. It is also famous for its size. In fact, Texas is so large that it takes about twelve hours to drive across it. For 114 years, Texas was the largest state in the United States. In 1959, however, Alaska became the forty-ninth and largest state. Proud Texans were upset, so they joked that because Alaska was mainly ice, it could melt. According to them, Texas was still the biggest state.

(84 words)

D Using synonyms

1 Work with a partner. For each item in the list below, find a similar word or phrase in the dictation paragraph. Then work with your class to rephrase the sentences using the new phrase or word.

1 *since*

4 *everywhere*

2 *remained*

5 *did not like this at all*

3 *in their opinion*

6 *well known*

2 Rewrite the dictation paragraph, making the substitutions that you discussed.

3 When you are finished, add your work to your portfolio.

E Self-correcting dictation

Cover the phrase or sentence below each line. Write on the line as your teacher dictates. Then, when your teacher says to check, uncover the words and check your writing.

1 _____

The Proud State of Texas

2 _____

Texas is well known around the world.

3 _____

It has oil wells, cattle ranches, and cowboys.

4 _____

Because of its size, it takes about twelve hours to drive across the state.

5 _____

Alaska became the forty-ninth and biggest state in 1959.

6 _____

Texans joked Alaska could melt because it was mainly ice.

F Editing practice

Rewrite these sentences correctly, using the editing symbols as a guide. (The editing symbols are explained in Appendix 4 on page 149.)

1 Because of its size, ⓢ takes about twelve hour # to drive across *art.* state.

2 Alaska *vt* become the four-ninth • *wf* and biggest state on *ww* 1959.

3 Texas ⓥ famous *prep* cowboy and oil. #

4 Texas *wf* ⌐always are⌐ joking about Alaska, because it *p* mainly ⓥ ice *p*

5 It *sv agr* take almost twelve hours to drive from east *c* texas *c* to west *c* texas. *c*

6 Texas *sv agr* border four other states *ww* who are Louisiana, Arkansas, Oklahoma, *conj* New Mexico.

7 Texans ⓥ proud *prep* their state.

8 ⓢ Is an interested *wf* place to visit.

G Dictation, Version 2

1 Study Dictation, Version 1 carefully to prepare for Dictation, Version 2, which is a variation of Version 1.

2 Write Version 2 of the dictation paragraph as your teacher dictates. Give your paper to your teacher to check, or check your work as your teacher directs. (The script for the teacher is in Appendix 2.)

14.2 Paragraph to essay

In this section, you will see how a paragraph can be expanded into an essay. An essay is a longer piece of writing that has several paragraphs. People often write essays for school or business purposes.

A Analyzing a paragraph

1 Read the travel paragraph called "Texas: More Than Cowboys and Oil Wells" on the following page. Answer these questions with your class.

1 What is the main idea of the paragraph?

2 What are the three points about Texas in the paragraph?

3 What is the difference between the topic sentence and the concluding sentence?

Paragraph

Texas: More than Cowboys and Oil Wells

[1]Texas is known around the world for its cowboys and oil wells, but it has other interesting features. [2]The first one is its varied geography. [3]Texas is located at the intersection of several geographical regions. [4]It contains mountains, hills, plains, beaches, deserts, forests, palm trees, and orange groves. [5]The second interesting feature of Texas is its cultural heritage. [6]Today, travelers in Texas can easily find elements of the ranching and cowboy culture, the culture of the rural Old South, the cultures of German and Czech immigrants, and especially the culture and language of Mexico. [7]These elements are mixed in varying proportions with the generic culture of modern America. [8]The third interesting feature is the regional pride of Texans. [9]Many people think of themselves as Texans first and U.S. citizens second. [10]This strong Texas identity is rooted in the history and size of Texas. [11]From 1836 to 1845, Texas was an independent country. [12]Then, after it became a state, it was the biggest in area for over 100 years. [13]Texans love to say that everything is bigger in Texas. [14]In conclusion, Texas has a unique flavor that comes from its varied geography, cultural heritage, and strong pride.

Texas: More than Cowboys and Oil Wells

[1]"Bang! Bang! Cowboy?" I often heard these words while traveling in Europe years ago when I said that I was from Texas. The next words were usually, "Do you have an oil well?" Although my home state is known around the world for its cowboys and oil wells, Texas has other interesting, though lesser known, features, which are its varied geography, its cultural heritage, and its strong pride.

[2]The first interesting feature of Texas is its varied geography. Texas is located at the intersection of several geographical regions. It has mountains, hills, plains, beaches, deserts, and forests. In one long day of driving, a person can start the morning beside rice fields in the humid southeastern part of the state and, in the evening, stop beside wild cactus plants in the dry western part. On a winter day, a person in the northern tip of Texas can be playing in the snow while another person in the southern tip is picking oranges near palm trees.

[3]The second interesting feature of Texas is its cultural heritage. The Institute of Texan Cultures, a museum in San Antonio, explains the cultural history of Texas and contains permanent exhibits on twenty-six cultural groups that helped build Texas. These groups range from Native Americans and Mexicans to Japanese and Chinese. Today, visitors to Texas can still see elements of the ranching and cowboy culture, the culture of the rural Old South, and the cultures of German and Czech immigrants, mixed with the generic culture of modern America. However, the past and the future of Texas are most closely associated with Mexico. For example, the 2000 census shows that about 28 percent of Texans speak Spanish in their homes, and this number is likely to grow.

[4]In addition to its geography and cultural heritage, the third interesting feature of Texas is the regional pride of its people. Supermarkets sell Texas-shaped pasta and people wear Texas-shaped earrings. Bumper stickers say, "Native-born Texan" and "I wasn't born in Texas, but I got here as fast as I could." Many people think of themselves as Texans first and as U.S. citizens second. This strong Texas identity is rooted in the history and size of Texas. From 1836 to 1845, Texas was an independent country. Then, after it became a state, it was the biggest in area for over 100 years, and Texans loved to say that everything was bigger in Texas. When Alaska became the forty-ninth and largest state in 1959, proud Texans joked that, because Alaska was mainly ice, it could melt. According to them, Texas was still the biggest state.

[5]In conclusion, Texas is an interesting place because of its varied geography, its cultural heritage, and the strong pride of its people. When I travel outside Texas or meet international visitors in Texas, I know the stereotypic images of Texas that they probably have. Therefore, I make sure to tell them that Texas is very diverse and has much more to see than cowboys and oil wells.

2 Find the following sentences in the paragraph on Texas. Write the sentence numbers in the blanks.

1 Topic sentence: _____

2 Sentences about geography: _____

3 Sentences about cultural background: _____

4 Sentences about regional pride: _____

5 Concluding sentence: _____

B Analyzing an essay

1 Read the file card about essays.

ESSAYS

An essay is a longer piece of writing that contains several paragraphs and focuses on one main idea. Because it is longer, an essay gives much more information about a topic than a paragraph.

An essay has three parts: the **introduction**, **body**, and **conclusion**.

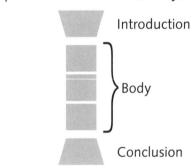

Introduction

Body

Conclusion

2 Read the essay on Texas, which is an expanded version of the paragraph. Write the paragraph numbers for each part.

1 Introduction: _____

2 Body: _____

3 Conclusion: _____

3 Reread the introduction and conclusion, and underline the sentence in each paragraph that gives the main idea of the essay.

4 What is the topic of each body paragraph? Discuss with your partner.

5 Discuss the purpose of the two anecdotes in the essay.

1 What is the first anecdote?

2 What is its purpose: to support an idea or to introduce a topic?

3 What is the second anecdote?

4 What is its purpose: to support an idea or to introduce a topic?

14.3 A travel paragraph

In this section, you will work with a small team on a travel project to an interesting geographic area.

A Developing a topic

1 With your class, discuss the list of geographic areas below. For each area, brainstorm specific places you could write about. Consult the map of the United States and other maps you have.

a States in the United States

b Famous cities in the United States

c Big cities in Asia

d Countries in Africa

e Tourist places in your city

f Nearby vacation places

UNITED STATES OF AMERICA

Scale of Miles
0   100   200   300

0   100 200 300 400
Scale of Kilometers

● State capital

★ Nation's capital

2 Form a team of three to six students. Choose a geographic area for your team. Then decide on individual places for each person to write about independently. Write your group's choices below.

My team's area	
My individual place	

3 Write some notes about what you already know about your place and what you want to know.

What I know	What I want to know

4 Share your notes with your team. Find out what other members of your team know about your individual place. Take notes as your group discusses your place.

5 Decide what additional information you need to get for your individual place. With your group, brainstorm possible sources for information.

 6 Do research on the Internet or at the library to find additional information. If possible, talk to someone from the geographic area you are researching.

B Planning your paragraph

1 Make a list of the well-known and less well-known features of the place you have researched.

Well-known features of _____	Less well-known features of _____

2 With your team, take turns telling about the features of the place you researched.

3 Choose three features to write about, and put a checkmark beside each one.

C Writing your paragraph

1 Write one paragraph about the three interesting features of the place you chose.

- Begin with a topic sentence.
- Write about *three* features (not two or four).
- Use enumeration signals to make your organization clear.
- Add sentences with supporting details to make each feature clear.
- End with a concluding sentence that restates the main idea.

2 After revising and editing, share your paragraph with your class.

14.4 Travel paragraph to essay

A Analyzing the body of an essay

1 Read the travel essay called "Texas: More than Cowboys and Oil Wells" on page 121.

2 Complete the outline below.

Outline

I.   Introduction

II. Varied Texas geography

    A. Geographical features

    B. Climates and plants

III. _____ of Texas

    A. Past cultures

    B. _____

    C. Future culture

IV. _____

    A. Texas products

    B. _____

    C. _____

V. Conclusion

B Writing the body of your essay

In this part, you will expand your paragraph from 14.3 into an essay. For each of the three features you wrote about in your paragraph, you will need to include supporting examples and facts.

1 Complete the outline below with your ideas.

Outline
I.   Introduction
II. First interesting feature _____
A. _____
B. _____
C. _____
III. Second interesting feature _____
A. _____
B. _____
C. _____
IV. Third interesting feature _____
A. _____
B. _____
C. _____
V.   Conclusion

 2 Use your outline to write the three body paragraphs of your essay.

C Writing an introduction

1 Read the file card.

INTRODUCTIONS

Every essay begins with an introduction.

Follow these steps for writing a good introduction.
* Write two or three sentences to focus the reader's attention on your topic.
* Write a final sentence that presents the main idea of the essay.

Here are two common types of introductions.
* One type may contain **background information** about the topic that will help the reader understand the main idea.
* Another type may contain an **anecdote** that is related to the topic and can help introduce the main idea.

2 Read these two introductions. Decide which one is a *background* introduction and which one is an *anecdote* introduction.

1 The United States consists of fifty states. Along with New York, Florida, and California, one of the most famous states in the United States is Texas. Although it is most famous for cowboys and oil wells, Texas has other interesting, but less famous, features. They are its varied geography, its cultural heritage, and its strong pride.

2 When I was traveling in Europe years ago, people often asked me where I was from. When I answered that I was from Texas, they often asked if I was a cowboy or owned an oil well. Although Texas is most famous for cowboys and oil wells, it has other interesting, but less famous, features. They are its varied geography, its cultural heritage, and its strong pride.

3 Underline the sentence in each introduction above that states the main idea of the essay.

4 Check your answer with the class.

5 Write an introduction for your essay, using either the *background* type or the *anecdote* type, as shown on the file card.

D Writing a conclusion

1 Read the following conclusions. Discuss which conclusion goes with which introduction in C2.

1 In conclusion, Texas has interesting geography, a varied cultural background, and a strong sense of pride about itself. These features, however, were rarely known to people I met in Europe. Therefore, after we talked about cowboys and oil wells, I often told them much more about my home state. Still, even today, I remember the words, "Bang! Bang! Cowboy?"

2 In summary, Texans are very proud of their state with its varied geography and interesting culture. These features are much less famous than its cowboy heritage and oil wells. All of these features, however, help people all over the world recognize Texas as one of the most famous of the United States.

2 Read the file card below.

CONCLUSIONS

Follow these steps for writing a good conclusion.
• Begin your conclusion with a conclusion signal (see below for examples).
• Restate the main idea. Do not use the same words as those in your introduction, but make some changes in grammar and vocabulary.
• Add a comment that is appropriate to your conclusion. If you wrote an anecdote in your introduction, add a comment about it. Or, if you gave background information in your introduction, add a comment about this information.

Here are some signals that you can use at the beginning of your conclusion.
In conclusion, . . .
In summary, . . .
In short, . . .

3 Reread the conclusions in D1. In each conclusion, circle the conclusion signal, and underline the sentence that restates the main idea.

4 Write a conclusion for your essay.

E Assembling and sharing your essay

1 Combine your introduction, body, and conclusion into an essay.

2 Work with your teacher and your team to revise and edit your travel essay.

3 With your team, display or publish your group's travel essays.

14.5 Independent-practice portfolio writing

1 Work with a partner or small group. Talk about the topics in the box.

2 Choose a topic from the box to write about in class or as homework. Focus on communicating your ideas. Do not worry about mistakes while you are writing, but be sure to reread and edit when you finish.

- Use good format and paragraph structure.
- Spend 15–30 minutes writing.
- Write 100–200 words.

Topics

Thinking about places of interest

1 A place you want to visit someday
2 A place you never want to see again
3 Your favorite place when you were younger
4 The beach

Looking inside and outside yourself

5 How you feel about your writing progress in this course
6 Your plans after this course is finished
7 Automobiles in the future
8 A topic from the list on page 148

---

3 When you are finished, add your work to your portfolio.

4 Review all of your independent-practice portfolio writing. Choose one of your favorites to revise and edit for sharing in a class publication project.

Appendix 1 The Mini-Handbook

This mini-handbook contains explanations and exercises. It begins with the alphabet. It then deals with larger and larger elements, from words and phrases to sentences and paragraphs. It ends with punctuation. You can use all or parts of the mini-handbook, and you can work with it in any order you choose.

A The alphabet

Printing

- There are two forms of each printed letter: capital and lower-case.
- People often use printing to fill out forms.
- Printing is the first type of writing that U.S. children learn.

Aa Bb Cc Dd Ee Ff Gg Hh Ii Jj
Kk Ll Mm Nn Oo Pp Qq Rr Ss Tt
Uu Vv Ww Xx Yy Zz

Cursive

- There are two forms of each cursive letter: capital and lower-case.
- People often use cursive for personal letters, school papers, and signatures.
- People in the United States begin to use cursive at the age of 8 or 9.

Aa Bb Cc Dd Ee Ff Gg Hh
Ii Jj Kk Ll Mm Nn Oo
Pp Qq Rr Ss Tt Uu Vv
Ww Xx Yy Zz

1 Practice saying the 26 letters of the English alphabet in order. Practice saying the name of these vowels: a, e, i, o, u.

2 Write the sentence below two times – first in cursive and then in print. Compare your letters with those in the box.

Good handwriting helps the reader.

1 _____

2 _____

3 Take turns with a partner spelling these words clearly so that your partner can write them correctly. Be sure to tell your partner when a capital letter is required.

1 quick _____   4 friend _____   7 business _____

2 July _____   5 above _____   8 Mexico _____

3 person _____   6 white _____

B Parts of speech

English has nine types of words that are called **parts of speech**:

noun (n.)	adverb (adv.)	preposition (prep.)
pronoun (pro.)	adjective (adj.)	conjunction (conj.)
verb (v.)	article (art.)	interjection (interj.)

Some words can function as more than one part of speech.
Everyone needs *love* (n.)
I *love* (v.) you.

1 Here are explanations and examples of each part of speech. Write additional examples of each one. Check your answers in your dictionary.

1 A noun is the name of a person, place, thing, or idea.
teacher, island, computer, freedom _____

2 A pronoun is a word that replaces a noun or refers to a noun.
we, him, their, mine _____

3 A verb expresses an action or a state of being.
write, are, seem _____

4 Adverbs modify verbs, adjectives, or other adverbs. They tell how, how often, when, and where.
quickly, never, daily, upstairs, very _____

5 Adjectives modify nouns and pronouns. They tell which, what kind of, how many, or how much.
first, comfortable, three, many _____

6 Articles also modify nouns. The two types of articles are definite and indefinite.
the _____

7 Prepositions show relationships between nouns and other words. They indicate such things as direction, location, time, or possession.
from, next to, during, of _____

8 Conjunctions are used to connect words or groups of words.
and, so _____

9 Interjections are used to express surprise or other strong emotions.
Wow! Hey! _____

2 Identify the part of speech of the underlined words. Use the abbreviations in the box.

1 Ouch! My foot really hurts!

2 Brazil and Bolivia are in the southern hemisphere.

3 A friend of mine has an interesting name.

4 Last night, he had a bad dream.

5 I often dream about my brother.

C Phrases

A **phrase** is a group of words that function together but do not have both a subject and a verb and do not express a complete idea. There are many types, but here are three useful ones.

- A **noun phrase** is a noun and the words that complete its meaning.
    A new laptop computer is *a wonderful gift.*
- A **prepositional phrase** is a preposition and the words that follow and complete its meaning.
    Teenagers *around the world* use the Internet *instead of the library.*
- A **verb phrase** is all the words that complete the tense and meaning of the verb.
    The family *is eating* dinner now. They *do not answer* the phone during meals.

1 Underline the nine prepositional phrases in this paragraph.

The format of my first paper was bad. I did not put the title in the center of the top line. I started a sentence in the left margin. I wrote my name at the end of the paragraph and put the date under it. Because of these mistakes, I got a bad grade in format.

2 Underline the six noun phrases in this paragraph.

An ordinary, elderly woman stopped the famous robber. She got a large reward, and her young grandson got seven big balloons. In the end, everyone was happy, except the unsuccessful robber.

3 Underline the verbs (one word) and verb phrases (two or more words) in this paragraph.

Today isn't a good day. We do not have time for lunch. We also do not have time to check our e-mail. We wanted a better day. Tomorrow is going to be better.

D Sentences

A sentence is a group of words that expresses a complete idea. The main parts of a sentence are the subject and the verb. The **subject** names who or what the sentence tells about. The **verb** tells what the subject is or does. The subject usually comes before the verb.

These are sentences.

    s   v
    Parents love their children.

    s   v
    Winter lasts several months.

These are not sentences. They are phrases.
    is living in a small house
    people all over the world

Work with a partner. Put *S* in front of each item if it is a sentence. Put *P* if it is a phrase. If it is a phrase, identify what is needed to form a sentence: a subject, a verb, or both a subject and a verb.

_____ 1 Kangaroos live in Australia.

_____ 2 Seoul is the capital of South Korea.

_____ 3 Saw beautiful clouds in the sky.

_____ 4 I need a printer for my computer.

_____ 5 A very large black dog.

_____ 6 Sharks live in the ocean.

_____ 7 In the middle of the summer.

E Sentences with linking verbs and subject complements

> In these sentences, the verb is a **linking verb** (*be, become, appear, seem, look, feel, taste, smell*). A linking verb is followed by a subject complement.
>
>   s   v   sc
> Coffee is *a popular drink* internationally
>
>   s   v   sc
> Coffee smells *wonderful* in the morning.

1 Underline the subject, and circle the verb(s). Then put two lines under the subject complement.

1 Fred was a bad cook.

2 Last year he became a chef.

3 Now he appears comfortable in his kitchen.

4 His dishes look beautiful and taste delicious.

5 Everyone feels happy about Fred's meals.

2 Form sentences by filling in the blanks with subject complements.

1 Green tea is a _____

2 Green tea has become _____

3 Green tea tastes _____

4 The carpet in the new apartment seemed _____

5 The carpet in the old apartment smelled _____

F Sentences with *There is/are* and *Here is/are*

> In *There is/are* and *Here is/are* sentences, the subject comes after the verb. *There* and *here* are not the subjects. The real subject comes after the verb.
>
>   v   s
> There are *two children* in my family.
>
>   v   s
> Here are *my sisters.*

1 Underline the subject, and circle the verb in each sentence.

1 There are many types of restaurants in my city.

2 There is a fast food restaurant near my house.

3 There is a French restaurant downtown.

4 Here are the directions to the French restaurant.

5 Here is the restaurant menu.

2 Fill in the blanks to complete these sentences.

1 There are _____ in my country.

2 There is _____ near here.

3 There is _____ in the street.

4 Here is _____ .

5 Here are _____ .

G Sentences with direct objects

Many sentences have transitive verbs. These verbs are followed by a **direct object**.

   s   v   do

Liz eats *lunch* at her desk.

      s   v   do   v   do

Later she takes *a break* and calls *some friends*.

1 Underline the subject, circle the verb, and put two lines under the direct object.

1 Many people use computers.

2 University students do research and write papers.

3 Their family, friends, and professors send e-mails.

4 Almost everyone sometimes plays a video game.

5 Computers serve many functions today.

2 Form sentences by filling in the blanks with direct objects.

1 Last night Pat and Kim watched _____ for hours.

2 They saw _____ between 6 pm and 2 am.

3 On weekends, they rent _____ .

4 They invite _____ .

5 Together they eat _____ and drink _____ .

H Gerunds and gerund phrases in sentences

A **gerund** is the *-ing* form of a verb that is used as a noun. A **gerund phrase** is a gerund plus all the words that follow to complete its meaning

A gerund or gerund phrase can function in several ways.

- Subject
     Walking is good exercise.
     Walking fast is good exercise.
- Subject complement
     Fred's favorite form of exercise is *walking*.
     Fred's favorite form of exercise is *walking in the park*.
- Direct object
     Fred enjoys *walking*.
     Fred enjoys *walking his dog*.
- Object of a preposition
     Fred gets lots of exercise by *walking*.
     Fred gets lots of exercise by *walking to school*.

1 Underline the gerunds and gerund phrases, and identify their functions (subject, subject complement, direct object, or object of a preposition).

1 Swimming uses many muscles.

2 Swimming laps builds cardiovascular health

3 Athletes train by swimming laps for hours.

4 Retired people often enjoy swimming laps for exercise.

5 Swimming does not strain your joints.

2 Underline the four gerund phrases in this paragraph.

> People today have three good ways of staying in touch with relatives and friends. The first way is writing letters. The second way is making phone calls. The third way is sending e-mail messages. Therefore, there is really no technological reason for people not to communicate.

I Forms that function as subject, subject complement, and objects

> The subject, subject complement or object of a sentence can take the form of a noun, noun phrase, pronoun, gerund, or gerund phrase.
>
> | | Subject | Subject complement | Direct object |
> |---|---|---|---|
> | **N** | *Austin* is great. | My hometown is *Austin*. | Everyone likes *Austin*. |
> | **NP** | *Big cities* are noisy. | Tokyo and Seoul are *big cities*. | Tourists enjoy *big cities*. |
> | **Pro** | *You* are funny | The funny person is *you*. | Everyone likes *you*. |
> | **G** | *Traveling* is fun. | My hobby is *traveling*. | I love *traveling*. |
> | **GP** | *Traveling by bus* is cheap. | His preference is *traveling by bus*. | She likes *traveling by bus*. |

1 Underline the subject, circle the verb, and put two lines under the complement or direct object. Then identify which form is used in each position.

1 Austin is the music capital of Texas.

2 Listening to live music is popular in Austin.

3 Musicians enjoy playing in Austin.

4 *South by Southwest* is a popular music festival in Austin.

5 Many music lovers attend this festival.

6 Listening is a real pleasure.

2 Write a sentence with each structure as the subject.

1 N   Music _____

2 NP   Classical music _____

3 Pro   It _____

4 G   Listening _____

5 GP   Playing the violin _____

J Simple sentences

> **Simple sentences** have one subject-verb combination, called a main (independent) clause. A simple sentence can have more than one subject and/or more than one verb in the subject-verb combination.
>
>   ˢ   ᵛ
> *Grammar is* easy for me.
>
>   ˢ¹   ˢ²   ᵛ
> *Grammar* and *mathematics are* easy for me.
>
>   ˢ   ᵛ¹   ᵛ²
> My little *brother likes* grammar but *doesn't like* mathematics.
>
>   ˢ¹   ˢ²   ˢ³   ᵛ¹   ᵛ²
> My *brother, sister,* and *cousin like* grammar but *don't like* math.
>
> ᵛ¹   ˢ   ᵛ¹
> *Does* your *roommate like* grammar and math?

1 In these simple sentences, mark the subjects and verbs as shown in the box.

1 Summer is my favorite season.

2 People enjoy outdoor sports during the summer.

3 Fall and spring seem more and more beautiful every year.

4 The falling leaves and the changing colors are beautiful.

5 In the spring, the trees and the smaller plants get new leaves.

6 Baseball and soccer are popular on warm spring days.

7 Do your friends ski and skate in the winter?

8 Skiing and snowboarding are dangerous sports and sometimes cause injuries.

> Simple sentences often contain **prepositional phrases**, which may be located at the beginning of the sentence, between the subject and verb, or after the verb.
>
> | Prep phrase | Subject | Prep phrase | Verb | Prep phrase |
> |---|---|---|---|---|
> | *After lunch* | a man | *with his young son* | rushed | *into the bank.* |
> | *With a quick step* | a woman | *together with her son* | walked | *in the rain.* |
> | *In a rush* | a mother | *along with her son* | ran | *up the street.* |

2 In these sentences, mark the subject and verb, and underline the prepositional phrases.

1 At this university, all students in English classes buy their books from the bookstore.

2 Before Friday, every class with a new teacher must go to the bookstore.

3 Each book with a map on the cover contains many photos and costs over $70.

4 The man and woman next to my roommates in the photos taught English in Mexico.

5 The man with a boy on his shoulders comes from Italy.

K Compound sentences

> Two simple sentences (main clauses) form a compound sentence when joined by a coordinating conjunction. These coordinating conjunctions are called **FANBOYS** because their first letters spell out this word. The activities in this book provide practice with only three – *and, but,* and *so* – but examples of all seven are presented here.
>
> Notice that you must put a **comma** before the coordinating conjunction.
>
> **For** Pete plays soccer well, *for* he practices every afternoon. (cause)
>
> **And** Dogs bark, *and* cats meow. (addition)
>
> **Nor** Carol doesn't speak Japanese, *nor* does she speak Portuguese. (negative alternatives)
>
> **But** Birds have feathers, *but* fish have fins. (contrast)
>
> **Or** You practice writing every day, *or* your writing does not improve. (alternatives)
>
> **Yet** Fred has plenty of money, *yet* he never buys new clothes. (contrast)
>
> **So** The rain was heavy, *so* we ran into the house. (result)

1 Mark the subjects, verbs, and direct objects (if any) in these compound sentences, and underline the comma and conjunction in each one.

            s   v   do   s   v   do

Example: New cars cost a lot of money, <u>but</u> they have many nice features.

1 Some people want large cars, but others want small, economical cars.

2 People have varied tastes, so carmakers manufacture many models.

3 Customers enjoy driving new cars, and car dealers encourage test drives.

4 Fuel economy and good handling are important features, but customers like up-to-date styling, too.

5 Buying a new car is stressful, so customers usually bring friends or family for support.

2 Combine the simple sentences, and rewrite as a compound sentence. Use *and, but,* or *so*.

1 Racing bikes have narrow tires. Mountain bikes have wide tires.

2 Mountain bikes travel off the trail. They need wider, softer tires.

3 Wide tires provide softness. Narrow tires provide speed.

3 Put an *S* for simple sentences and *C* for compound sentences.

_____ 1 Extreme sports are dangerous and attract many young people.

_____ 2 Extreme sports are dangerous, but some people enjoy them.

_____ 3 Extreme sports and other risky activities cause many injuries.

_____ 4 Some people like risky activities, and others avoid all risks.

_____ 5 Skydiving and snowboarding are popular among young people.

L Complex sentences

A **simple** sentence has one main clause, a **compound** sentence has two main clauses connected by a coordinating conjunction, and a **complex** sentence has at least one main clause and one subordinate clause. A subordinate clause must be joined to a main clause to form a sentence.

Simple sentences with one main clause (MC)
Texas is hot in July.
My cat got wet yesterday.
Your words were very kind.

Subordinate clauses (SC)
because you like hot weather
when it rained
what you said

1 Mark the main clauses with *MC,* and mark the subordinate clauses with *SC.* For each MC, add a capital letter at the beginning and a period or question mark at the end.

_____ 1 flowers bloom in the spring

_____ 2 if your backpack is full of books

_____ 3 while I waited in line at the bank

_____ 4 good spelling is important to a writer

_____ 5 hamsters make good pets

_____ 6 before World War II ended

_____ 7 when I hear my phone ring

_____ 8 it is hard to find a parking place

_____ 9 what he ate

_____ 10 what did he eat

2 Underline each main clause, and label it *MC.* Put two lines under the subordinate clause, and label it *SC.*

1 Cookbooks that have many color photographs are often bestsellers.

2 What readers enjoy are the color photographs.

3 When publishers do not include color photographs, their cookbooks rarely sell well these days.

4 Readers like photographs because they show how the food looks.

5 Everyone knows that beautiful cookbooks are expensive.

6 The cook who wrote the new cookbook is quite famous.

3 Read each sentence, and mark *S* for simple sentences, *C* for compound sentences, and *CX* for complex sentences.

_____ 1 The dogs are under the house.

_____ 2 Computers are useful, but they often crash.

_____ 3 My mother won't tell what her weight is.

_____ 4 Cleopatra, who ruled Egypt, died long ago.

_____ 5 Ice cream would be good for dessert, but this restaurant doesn't have any.

_____ 6 Whoever kissed Bill left lipstick on his cheek.

_____ 7 That your roommate is Japanese surprises me.

_____ 8 Monica enjoys walking in the park.

_____ 9 I like cookies, but I do not want any now.

_____ 10 The cookies that you left on the table are all gone now.

M Types of subordinate clauses

There are three types of subordinate clauses. **Adjective clauses** modify nouns and begin with words like *who, whom, whose, which,* or *that.* **Adverb clauses** begin with adverbial conjunctions, such as *after, before, if, unless, because,* and *although.* **Noun clauses** function in the place of a noun and begin with *that, whether,* or a wh-question word, such as *who, why, how, where,* and *when.*

Note that, when an adverb clause comes before the main clause, a comma must separate the subordinate adverb clause from the main clause. When it comes after the main clause, there is no comma.

- Adjective clauses
  I did not see the man *who helped you.*
- Adverb clauses
  After I have breakfast, I generally check my email.
  I generally check my email *after I have breakfast.*
- Noun clauses
  That *you cry at sad movies* does not surprise me.

These sentences have a main clause and a subordinate clause. Underline the subordinate clause, and mark it *ADJ* if it is an adjective clause, *ADV* if it is an adverb clauses, or *N* if it is a noun clause.

1 After I finished, I left the room.

2 What you wrote was nice.

3 I like what you wrote.

4 The students who lost their folders are upset.

5 Peter sings while Mary dances.

6 If Paul sings, Mary will dance.

7 I know what Paul will sing.

8 I will go if you will go

9 Dogs chase cats when they can.

10 She never sings although she has a nice voice.

N Paragraphs and the position of topic sentences

Each paragraph in English should have one main idea, which is usually stated in a sentence called the **topic sentence**. When you read in English, you will find the topic sentence in various positions in paragraphs, as described below.

Deductive organization
When the topic sentence is at or near the beginning of the paragraph, the paragraph has deductive organization. Deductive organization is good in formal academic and professional writing because the main idea is clear to the reader from the beginning.

xxxxxxxxxxxxxxxxxxxxxxxxxxxxxxx
xxxxxxxxxxxxxxxxxxxxxxxxxxxxxxx
xxxxxxxxxxxxxxxxxxxxxxxxxxxxxx.

Inductive organization
When the topic sentence is at or near the end of the paragraph, the paragraph has inductive organization. Inductive organization is useful in writing stories, especially mysteries, and in explaining a new idea or theory.

xxxxxxxxxxxxxxxxxxxxxxxxxxxxxx
xxxxxxxxxxxxxxxxxxxxxxxxxxxxxxx
xxxxxxxxxxxxxxxxxxxxxxxxxxxxxxx.

Deductive-restatement organization

When the topic sentence is at the beginning and restated at the end, the paragraph has deductive-restatement organization. This type of organization is very good in formal writing, especially in essays, because the reader has two chances to understand the main idea.

xxxxxxxxxxxxxxxxxxxxxxxxxxxxxxxx
xxxxxxxxxxxxxxxxxxxxxxxxxxxxxxxx
xxxxxxxxxxxxxxxxxxxxxxxxxxxxxxxx.

Implied main idea

When there is no topic sentence, the main idea is implied. This type of organization gives all the supporting information but does not state the main idea. Therefore, it is not popular in U.S. education or business.

xxxxxxxxxxxxxxxxxxxxxxxxxxxxxxx
xxxxxxxxxxxxxxxxxxxxxxxxxxxxxxx
xxxxxxxxxxxxxxxxxxxxxxxxxxxxxxx.

Match each paragraph to one of the four types of paragraph organization.

a inductive   b deductive   c deductive-restatement   d implied

1 _____ People today have three good ways of staying in touch with relatives and friends. The first good way is writing letters. The second way is making phone calls. The third way is sending e-mail.

2 _____ People today have three good ways of staying in touch with relatives and friends. The first good way is writing letters. The second way is making phone calls. The third way is sending e-mail messages. Therefore, there is really no technological reason for people not to stay in touch.

3 _____ Writing letters is a good way of staying in touch with relatives and friends. It is the oldest way. A second good way is making phone calls. This way is very popular. A third way of staying in touch is sending e-mail messages. This is the newest way and is more popular each year.

4 _____ The first good way of staying in touch with relatives and friends is writing letters. The second way is making phone calls. The third way is sending e-mail messages. People today have three good ways of staying in touch with relatives and friends.

O Capitalization

In English, capital letters are used in many very specific ways. Three ways are given in the file card on page 12. Here are some of the other ways.

- Capitalize the pronoun I:
  It is *I* who called you.
- Capitalize proper nouns (the names of specific persons, places, or things): *Einstein, Brazil, the Brooklyn Bridge, the Titanic.*
- Capitalize the names of languages, religions, and nationalities: *English, Islam, the Japanese.*
- Capitalize the names of specific family members: *Uncle Joe, Grandma Lizzie* but *your uncle, my grandmother.*
- Capitalize the names of months, days of the week, and holidays: *January, Tuesday, Halloween.*
- Capitalize the names of schools, courses, and departments: *Florida State University, English 301, the Computer Science Department* but *the field of computer science.*
- Use capital letters in abbreviations: *the TOEFL, the U.N., the U.S.A., a B.S. degree, an M.A. degree, a Ph.D., Mr., Ms., and Dr.*

Rewrite these sentences, using capital letters appropriately.

1 my boyfriend and I loved the movie called titanic.

2 the book called harry potter and the sorcerers stone was popular in 2001.

3 elizabeth will take the toefl on monday.

4 mr. smith's mother is living in the u.s.

5 charles wants to get an m.a. degree or a ph.d. degree at the university of michigan.

6 after i talked to professor jones, i went to the library to study english.

P Punctuation marks and other symbols

Here are the names of some of the **punctuation marks and other symbols** used in English.

1	.	a period	8	don't		an apostrophe
2	,	a comma	9	well-done		a hyphen
3	?	a question mark	10	and/or		a slash
4	!	an exclamation point	11	[ ]		brackets
5	" "	quotation marks	12	( )		parentheses
6	:	a colon	13	Li@ny.net		at
7	;	a semi-colon	14	yahoo.com		dot

1 Read the paragraph in the box and rewrite it, adding punctuation and other symbols as instructed.

For Both Children and Adults

I read Harry Potter and the Sorcerers Stone by J K Rowling recently Have you read it I was very surprised that I liked it so much I knew it was a childrens book and Im not a child anymore I think Rowling is a good author because both adults and children enjoy her books

1 Draw a line under the name of the book.

2 Put periods after the initials of the author.

3 Find the contraction, and add an apostrophe

4 Find the two possessive words, and add apostrophes.

5 How many sentences are there? _____ Add a period or question mark after each sentence.

6 One of the sentences needs a comma because it is a compound sentence. Find this sentence, and insert the comma.

Commas are used to separate items in a list or series of three or more things. A list of three items needs two commas, a list of four items needs three commas, and so on.

                                        1   2   3   4

My mother's vegetable soup contains potatoes, carrots, onions, and celery.

1 2   3   1   2   3

Pat, Kim, and Ann enjoy watching videos, eating chips, and staying up late.

2 Read each sentence, find the list, count the items, and add commas in the appropriate places.

1 She loves to put strawberries raspberries or blueberries on her morning cereal.

2 Careful writers plan carefully write several drafts make many revisions and do careful editing when they are writing important papers.

3 With no time money or energy left she sat down on a park bench and cried.

4 It is easy to meet new people in a dorm at a coffee shop or in a chat room.

5 There are no windows tables or other facilities in his small cell.

3 Rewrite this paragraph, adding capital letters and the appropriate marks of punctuation.

> how frustrating yesterday was why did I even get up my bus was a half hour late I spilled coffee on my new white shirt the boss was in a terrible mood all day because her bus broke down on the way home in my apartment there was water everywhere but no electricity what a day

4 Commas are also used in compound sentences with *and, but,* and *so* (see item L) and in complex sentences where the subordinate clause comes before the main clause (see item M). Add commas to these sentences where necessary.

1 Halloween is next week so everyone needs a costume.

2 When people go to Halloween parties they wear costumes.

3 Some costumes are expensive but many wonderful ones are not.

4 Because people want to make jack-o-lanterns they buy pumpkins.

5 After you carve a pumpkin you put a candle inside.

6 People in the United States gather with their families when it is time for Thanksgiving dinner.

7 The adults enjoy talking and the children like to play.

8 Although turkey is the most popular food on Thanksgiving some families prefer beef or pork.

9 Some people watch a football game after dinner.

10 Turkeys are very big so many people have turkey sandwiches the day after Thanksgiving.

5 Joe had a ticket for a trip from Chicago to Toronto. Add punctuation to each paragraph about Joe to make the ending true.

?
Chicago

?
Toronto

> Joe walked into the plane before the flight attendant closed the door he walked out when the plane landed where was Joe he was in Toronto

> Joe walked into the plane before the flight attendant closed the door he walked out when the plane landed where was Joe he was still in Chicago

Appendix 2 Script

3.1 **Enumeration dictation, B1 Dictation, Version 1 (page 15)**
(The instructions in the box below should be used for all dictations. Read the words in bold, and follow the instructions in italics.)

Instructions for Dictations

- **Listen only. Do not write.** *(After saying this, read the whole dictation at near-native speed. Do not pause between the phrases marked with slashes.)*
- **Listen and write.** *(Now read the dictation, pausing between phrases marked with slashes. Give students time to write. Adjust the length of the pauses to fit your students' proficiency. Read each phrase no more than twice.)*
- **You have one minute to study your work.** *(You can adjust the time as necessary, depending on the length of the dictation and the proficiency of your students.)*
- **Listen again and check your work.** *(This time, read the whole dictation again at a slow but natural speed. Read complete sentences, pausing only slightly between the phrases.)*

Staying in Touch

People today / have three good ways / of staying in touch / with friends and relatives. / The first way / is writing letters. / The second way / is making phone calls. / The third way /is sending e-mail messages. / Therefore, there is really / no technological reason / for people not to communicate.   *(46 words)*

3.1 **Enumeration dictation, G2 Dictation, Version 2 (page 18)**
(Follow the instructions for dictations.)

Staying in Touch

Today there is really no reason / for people not to stay in touch / with friends and relatives. / They have three good ways / of communicating. / One way is telephoning. / The second way / is sending letters. / The third way / is writing e-mail messages. / Therefore, / staying in touch is easy.   *(47 words)*

3.2 **Student paper format, B1 Reviewing vocabulary about format (page 21)**
1 Write 1 in the upper left-hand <u>corner</u> of the paper.
2 Put 4 in the <u>upper</u> right-hand corner of the page.
3 Put 10 in the lower <u>left-hand</u> corner.
4 Write 7 in the <u>lower</u> right-hand corner.
5 Put 3 in the center of the <u>top</u> line.
6 Write 8 in the middle of the <u>bottom</u> line.
7 Write 11 on the left <u>margin</u> line in the center of the page.
8 Put 6 in the right margin in the <u>middle</u> of the page.

4.2 **Writing a story, A1 Introduction to the story (page 26)**

It is an ordinary day at the First National Bank. A woman and her grandson are in the bank. The woman has a handbag and an umbrella on her arm. The boy has a balloon on a string. The woman begins to make a deposit and cash a check. Then a man with a hat walks in. The man slowly walks to a window. He suddenly pulls out a gun. He gives the teller a note. He gets two bags of money from her. He starts to run away. The woman quickly starts to run after him. She hits him hard with her umbrella. She stops him. A policeman immediately takes the robber away. A crowd watches. The bank manager gives the woman a reward. She looks very happy. He gives the boy seven balloons. The boy also has a smile on his face. In the end, everyone is happy except the robber.

7.1 **Process dictation, B1 Dictation, Version 1 (page 56)**
(Follow the instructions for dictations.)

Steps in Getting a Driver's License

In the United States, / teenagers can get / a driver's license / before becoming 18 / by following three basic steps. / First, / they get a learner's permit / by taking a course / and a written exam / on traffic laws. /

Next, they practice driving / under adult supervision. / Finally, they take a driving test / for a regular license. / Following this three-step process / allows U.S. teenagers / to drive at a young age. *(65 words)*

7.1 **Process dictation, F2 Dictation, Version 2 (page 58)**
(Follow the instructions for dictations on page 142.)

Steps in Getting a Driver's License

Following a three-step process / allows U.S. teenagers / to drive before becoming 18. / First, they take a course / and a written test on traffic laws / to get a learner's permit. / Next, they practice driving / under the supervision / of an adult. / Finally, / they take a driving test / to get a regular license. / By following three basic steps, / U.S. teenagers can drive / at a young age. *(63 words)*

8.2 **Math terms, A Numbers (page 65)**
(Before starting the dictation, write the items and given numbers on the board, transparency, or big piece of paper so that you can point to them as needed.)

1 Listen to me read the numbers. Fill in the missing numbers you hear.

1	1.5	5	½	9	¾
2	1.57	6	1½	10	⁵⁄₄
3	1.572	7	11½	11	12¾
4	98.6	8	¼	12	⅔

2 We're going to practice with the numbers in the list. Follow my instructions. Ready?

a First, I'm going to say a number. Say the item number that you see beside that number. *(Say the numbers in random order.)*

b Now, read the number that I point to. *(Point to the numbers in random order.)*

c Finally, I'm going to say an item number. Read the number beside it. *(Say the item numbers in random order.)*

8.2 **Math terms, E2 Tables, ranges, and averages (page 67)**

1 Linda carries a backpack. The person who carries a backpack is Linda.
2 Tom carries a duffel bag. He puts his books and papers in a duffel bag.
3 Kathy carries a tote bag. The person who carries a tote bag is Kathy.
4 John carries a briefcase. He puts his books and papers in a briefcase.
5 The briefcase costs $55. The price of the briefcase is $55.
6 The duffel bag weighs 1.5 pounds. The weight of the duffel bag is 1.5 pounds.
7 The height of the backpack is 17 inches. The backpack is 17 inches high.
8 The width of the tote bag is 15 inches. The tote bag is 15 inches wide.
9 The depth of the briefcase is 3½ inches. The briefcase is 3½ inches deep.
10 The backpack weighs 1 pound. The weight of the backpack is 1 pound.

9.1 **Ms. Lee's daily routine, A1 Learning vocabulary (page 74)**
Liz gets up. She takes a shower. She gets dressed. She listens to the news while she makes her lunch. She takes the bus to work. She stops at a stand to pick up coffee and a snack. She gets to the office and says hello. She checks her e-mail. She does paperwork and goes to meetings. She has lunch at her desk. She works at her computer and sees clients. She returns telephone calls. She gets off work. She gets together with friends or works out at the gym. She goes to bed. She dreams about the weekend and her next vacation.

9.1 **Ms. Lee's daily routine, A2 Learning vocabulary (page 74)**
A She takes the bus to work.
B She takes a shower.
C She works at her computer and sees clients.
D She dreams about the weekend and her next vacation.
E She does paperwork and goes to meetings.
(Stop and check answers. A, picture 5; B, picture 2; C, picture 11; D, picture 16; E, picture 9)
F She gets to the office and says hello.
G Liz gets up.
H She goes to bed.

I She gets off work.

J She listens to the news while she makes her lunch.

(Stop and check answers. F, picture 7; G, picture 1; H, picture 15; I, picture 13; J, picture 4.)

K She checks her e-mail.

L She gets together with her friends or works out at the gym.

M She gets dressed.

N She returns telephone calls.

O She eats lunch at her desk.

P She stops at a stand to pick up coffee and a snack.

(Stop and check answers. K, picture 8; L, picture 14; M, picture 3; N, picture 12; O, picture 10; P, picture 6.)

11.1 **Classification dictation, B1 Dictation, Version 1 (page 91)**
(Follow the instructions for dictations on page 142.)

Advice about Dictionaries

People studying English / usually want a dictionary. / There are three main types / to consider. / One main type / is a bilingual dictionary. Another main type / is a dictionary for learners of English. / Still another main type / is a dictionary / for native speakers of English. / Therefore, before buying, / students should think carefully / about which of these three main types / is best for them. *(61 words)*

11.1 **Classification dictation, F2 Dictation, Version 2 (page 93)**
(Follow the instructions for dictations on page 142.)

Advice about Dictionaries

Students of English / should think carefully / about several types of dictionaries / before buying one. / Three types to consider / are bilingual dictionaries, / dictionaries for learners of English, / and dictionaries for native speakers. / People studying English / should buy / the best type of dictionary for them. *(43 words)*

12.1 **Getting some exercise, 2 (page 99)**
(First, lead the class through the activity by reading the instructions and acting them out with the students as you go. Then, if desired, read the instructions again, having students follow the instructions without your lead. Finally, for additional listening practice, try reading the instructions in random order for the students to follow.)

1 Stand up. S-t-r-e-t-c-h.

2 Take a deep breath. Hold it. Breathe out. *(Repeat.)*

3 Turn your head slowly to the left. Turn your head slowly to the right. Face forward.

4 Lift your right foot. Gently bend your right knee. Put your foot down.

5 Lift your left foot. Gently bend your left knee. Put your foot down.

6 Rise up on your toes. Put your feet flat on the floor. *(Repeat 2 times.)*

7 Rub your lower back.

8 Raise both hands over your head. Bend both elbows. Reach down and rub the back of your neck.

9 Put both hands on your hips. Twist your trunk slowly from side to side. Face forward.

10 Move your eyes to the right, and then to the left. Look across the room and then at your feet. *(Repeat 2 times.)*

11 Alternately, lift your feet 6 inches and walk in place for 10 seconds.

12 Raise both arms level with your shoulders. Lower your arms close to your sides. Raise and lower your arms 8 times.

13 Rotate your wrists 8 times.

14 Smile. Laugh. Frown. Smile.

15 Make fists. Shake your fists. Slowly open your hands. *(Repeat.)*

16 Take a deep breath. Hold it. Breathe out. *(Repeat.)*

17 Shake hands with someone nearby. S-t-r-e-t-c-h. Sit down.

12.2 **Sentence combining, A1 Getting ready (page 100)**

1 What do people with sedentary jobs need?

2 How many people find ways to get enough exercise?

3 Does the second person or the third person stretch beside the workstation?

12.2 Sentence combining, A2 Getting ready (page 100)

Exercise for Busy People

Although exercise is important for everyone, not everyone gets enough. More and more people have sedentary jobs and rarely use their large muscles. Although these workers sometimes get exercise on sunny weekends, they need easy ways to get exercise every day. They can learn some easy ways from these three people and have healthier lives. The first person, a very important lawyer, has a nice car, but she walks to work every day. Although she wears an elegant suit under her coat, she has old jogging shoes on her feet. She carries her dressy shoes in her briefcase because she wants to keep them clean. The second person, a successful accountant, drives her car to work, so she adds physical activity to her daily routine in a different way. She parks her car very far from her office building and takes the stairs instead of the elevator. She also walks with co-workers during lunch and often stands up while making phone calls. The third person, a computer programmer, exercises his eyes every hour because he wants to avoid eyestrain and headaches. He also stands up and stretches beside his ergonomic computer workstation because he wants to prevent back pain. Because exercise is important to these three busy people, they find ways to get enough.

12.2 Sentence combining, A3 Getting ready (page 101)

1 What does the lawyer wear to work?

2 Where does the accountant park her car?

3 How often does the computer programmer exercise his eyes?

12.2 Sentence combining, A4 Getting ready (page 101)

(Again, read the paragraph Exercise for Busy People *given in A2 above.)*

12.3 Dictation: Why people exercise, A1 Dictation, Version 1 (page 102)

(Follow the instructions for dictations on page 142.)

Why People Exercise

Why do people exercise? / Some people exercise / for their cardiovascular health. / Other people exercise / for their appearance. / They try to burn more calories / because they want to lose weight / and look better. / Still other people exercise / for fun and relaxation. / In fact, / most people probably exercise / for all three reasons.   *(50 words)*

12.3 Dictation: Why people exercise, E2 Dictation, Version 2 (page 104)

(Follow the instructions for dictations on page 142.)

Why People Exercise

Why do people exercise? / Most people exercise / for three reasons. / They exercise / for relaxation and fun. / They exercise / for their cardiovascular health. / They also exercise / for their appearance / because they want to look better.   *(34 words)*

14.1 Dictation: The proud state of Texas, B1 Dictation, Version 1 (page 118)

(Follow the instructions for dictations on page 142.)

The Proud State of Texas

Texas is known / around the world / for its oil wells, / cattle ranches, / and cowboys. / It is also famous / for its size. / In fact, Texas is so large / that it takes about twelve hours / to drive across it. / For 114 years, / Texas was the largest state / in the United States. / In 1959, however, / Alaska became / the forty-ninth and largest state. / Proud Texans were upset, / so they joked / that because Alaska was mainly ice, / it could melt. / According to them, / Texas was still the biggest state.   *(84 words)*

14.1 Dictation: The proud state of Texas, G2 Dictation, Version 2 (page 120)

(Follow the instructions for dictations on page 142.)

The Proud State of Texas

Texas is famous / around the world / for its cowboys, / cattle ranches, / oil wells, and size. / It takes about thirteen hours / to drive across the state. / Because Texas was / the largest state in the United States / for 114 years, / Texans were upset / when Alaska became a state / in 1959. / They joked that it could melt / because it was mainly ice. / According to proud Texans, / Texas is still the largest state.   *(69 words)*

Appendix 3 Guide to the Portfolio Project

In this course, you will make a portfolio of writing assignments (see Unit 2, page 11 for how to get started). Use a folder or notebook with prongs or rings to keep all of your portfolio writing securely together.

Questions and answers about the portfolio project

What is the portfolio project?

For the portfolio project, you will keep a folder with a collection of your weekly assignments – some typed and some handwritten – from this book. There are two types of writing assignments for the portfolio project: guided-practice portfolio assignments and independent-practice portfolio assignments.

What are guided-practice portfolio assignments?

Guided-practice portfolio assignments are directly related to activities in the book. They are called *guided* because you are given words and sentences you need to do the writing. When you do guided-practice portfolio assignments, you should focus on accuracy. If you make too many mistakes, your teacher may ask you to rewrite and resubmit the assignment. There is a list of these assignments by unit on page 147.

What are independent-practice portfolio assignments?

Independent-practice assignments may or may not be directly connected with activities in the book. They are called *independent* because you will use your own language and vocabulary to express your own ideas. When you do this type of portfolio assignment, focus on communicating ideas clearly, writing the suggested number of words, and writing efficiently. In addition to the topics given at the end of each unit, your teacher may suggest a topic, or you may choose a topic from the list on page 148.

What is the difference between the portfolio project and the multi-draft compositions for publication?

Almost every unit has a group of activities that leads you to write, revise, edit, and share a major composition. For these compositions, you will write more than one draft. The book has many suggestions for publishing these multi-draft compositions. In addition, however, students need to do additional writing practice. The portfolio project is a collection of these weekly writing assignments.

What is the difference between a portfolio and a journal or diary?

Portfolios can contain many different types of writing assignments, but a journal or diary usually has only personal writing.

Why use a folder for the portfolio and not a spiral notebook?

You will be adding new papers to your portfolio each week. A folder has rings or prongs so you can add pages easily. You can be writing a new assignment while your teacher has your portfolio of previous assignments.

How about computers versus handwriting?

Learning to use the computer comfortably and efficiently is important for success in our increasingly computer-dependent world. Therefore, if possible, it is a good idea to write your portfolio assignments on the computer. However, a computer is not necessary for this course.

- *Computer format:* Use font size 12, with approximately 1-inch margins at the top and bottom and 1¼ inch margins on the sides. Always double space and write a title. Look at the format sample on page 20.
- *Handwriting format:* Use lined paper (preferably 8½" x 11") with margins. Always write a title. Look at the format sample on page 19.

How much should I write?

When doing portfolio assignments, you want to write fluently and efficiently and develop your writing "muscles." You want to develop confidence in your ability to write and to finish within a time limit. Your teacher will give you time and length requirements.

You will usually write one strong paragraph per topic (about 100 to 200 words) in about 15 to 30 minutes, either in class or at home. If you use a computer, the software can count words for you. If you write by hand, you will need to count.

What is a typical portfolio routine?

On a regular basis, perhaps once a week, students add assignments, perhaps one guided-practice and one independent-practice assignment, to their folders and turn them in. Some weeks, however, there may be more or fewer assignments, depending on other work on multi-draft compositions and/or the publication project.

Checklist of guided-practice portfolio assignments

This is a complete list of the guided-practice portfolio assignments. Put a checkmark beside the ones your teacher assigns.

_____ 1.2B Writing a letter about your partner (page 4)

_____ 1.4A Writing a letter to the teacher (page 6)

_____ 1.4B Writing a letter to the class (page 6)

_____ 2.5C Adding subjects and verbs to "My Twin Brothers" (page 14)

_____ 3.1E Adding support to the dictation "Staying in Touch" (page 17)

_____ 3.2C Correcting mistakes in format (page 23)

_____ 4.2E Adding descriptive details and rewriting a story in the past tense (page 30)

_____ 4.3B Changing the facts of a story (page 31)

_____ 4.4C Writing a letter or e-mail about the bank robbery (page 33)

_____ 7.1D Adding support to the dictation "Steps in Getting a Driver's License" (page 58)

_____ 7.2A Revising format and signal words in "Driver's License" (page 59)

_____ 8.3D Writing "Meet Writing 310" (page 70)

_____ 8.4A Revising "California in 2000" to group information (page 70)

_____ 9.2C Writing complex sentences in "Ms. Lee's Daily Routine" (page 77)

_____ 9.3B Using editing symbols to revise a paragraph (page 78)

_____ 11.1D Adding support to the dictation "Advice about Dictionaries" (page 93)

_____ 11.3A Adding support to "Types of Computers in the Workplace" (page 94)

_____ 11.3B Using editing symbols to revise a paragraph (page 95)

_____ 12.2C Writing "Exercise for Busy People" with longer sentences (page 101)

_____ 12.3C Adding support to the dictation "Why People Exercise" (page 103)

_____ 12.5A Revising enumeration signals in "Why People Exercise" (page 105)

_____ 12.5B Using editing symbols to revise a paragraph (page 105)

_____ 13.3E Using editing symbols to revise a paragraph (page 115)

_____ 14.1D Using synonyms in the dictation "The Proud State of Texas" (page 119)

Additional topics for independent-practice portfolio writing

If you don't want to use the topics in the units, you can choose additional topics from the boxes or the list below. For example, the words from the three boxes, "A good experience in the past," might inspire you to write about your favorite vacation as a child.

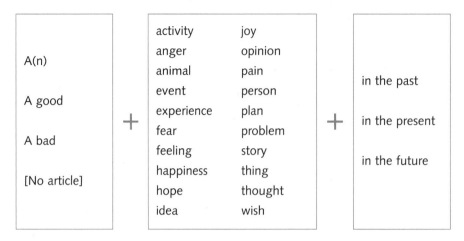

A(n)	+	activity	joy	+	in the past
A good		anger	opinion		
A bad		animal	pain		in the present
[No article]		event	person		
		experience	plan		in the future
		fear	problem		
		feeling	story		
		happiness	thing		
		hope	thought		
		idea	wish		

Here are some more topics to choose from.

A bad apartment	Education	My girlfriend/boyfriend
A big disappointment	Elvis	My hair
A big problem in my city	Feeling homesick	My messy/neat room
A city I have visited	Genetic engineering	My pet
A famous dead person	Global warming	My problems with English
A famous living person	Gossiping	My roommate(s)
A fantastic day	Guns	Next year I . . .
A good/bad president	I feel sad/good because . . .	Politics
A good/bad teacher	I hate . . .	Pollution
A good/bad way to learn English	I love . . .	Smoking
A great restaurant	Life at home	Space travel
A terrible/wonderful hobby	Life in the mountains	Stars
A terrible/wonderful neighbor	Life in the U.S.	Stress
After school I . . .	Motorcycles	Tattoos
AIDS	Movies are bad for kids because . . .	The desert
Bullies	Music	The Olympics
Cafeteria food	My ancestors	The person I want to marry
Children	My biggest fear	The World Cup
Clothing I like/hate to wear	My dream job	Traffic in my city
Coffee shops	My favorite holiday	TV is good/bad because . . .
Cooking	My favorite movie	War/peace
Dancing	My favorite possession	Whales
Dating	My first day here	When I was a child, I . . .
Diamonds	My (future/ex) wife/husband	Yesterday morning I . . .

Appendix 4 List of Editing Symbols

Over the years, writers and editors have developed editing symbols to help them communicate ideas about how a text needs to be changed. Teachers and students often use these symbols in the United States in both high schools and universities.

Introduction to editing symbols

1 Cover the symbol and explanation columns, and compare the sentences in the other columns. With your class, discuss the meaning of the editing symbol. Then, uncover the first columns to check your answer.

2 Work with a partner. Cover the fourth column, and use the information in the other three columns to write a corrected sentence. Then, check your sentence with the one in the last column.

List of editing symbols

Refer to this list whenever necessary in editing your work.

Symbol	Explanation	Sentence marked with symbols	Corrected sentence
1 ◯	Insert something	Beverly and Carol born in Texas.	Beverly and Carol were born in Texas.
2 ℘	Delete this	They are a good friends.	They are good friends.
3 s	Subject	Worked in Tunisia	Carol worked in Tunisia.
4 v	Verb	Carol also a lawyer.	Carol is also a lawyer.
5 vt	Verb tense error	Carol teach in Malaysia in 1986.	Carol taught in Malaysia in 1986.
6 pro agr	Pronoun agreement error	Carol always enjoys himself at parties.	Carol always enjoys herself at parties.
7 poss	Use possessive form	Beverly husband is a cyclist.	Beverly's husband is a cyclist.
8 sp	Spelling error	Beverly and Carol are teechers.	Beverly and Carol are teachers.
9 c ¢	Capitalization error	both of them like Languages.	Both of them like languages.
10 p ℘	Punctuation error	They both, speak French	They both speak French.
11 ⌢ ⌣	Connect and make one word	They like to work to gether.	They like to work together.
12 ww	Wrong word	Carol King lives at Austin, Texas.	Carol King lives in Austin, Texas.
13 wf	Right word, but wrong form	Both of them enjoy teach.	Both of them enjoy teaching.
14 #	Number error, singular – plural	They met over 30 year ago.	They met over 30 years ago.

Symbol	Explanation	Sentence marked with symbols	Corrected sentence
15 *sv agr*	Subject-verb agreement error	*sv agr* Beverly have three kids and two grandkids.	Beverly has three kids and two grandkids.
16	Word order error	They taught in Algeria English classes.	They taught English classes in Algeria.
17 *rep*	Repetition	*rep* Every day Carol has coffee daily.	Carol has coffee every day.
18 *ind* →	Indent here	xxxxxxxxxxxxxxxxxxxxxxxx xxxxx. xxxxxxxxxxxxxxxxxx. *ind* xxxxxxxxxxxxxxxxxxxxxxxx xxxxxxxxxxxxxxx.	xxxxxxxxxxxxxxxxxxxxxxxx xxxxxx. xxxxxxxxxxxxxxxxxx. xxxxxxxxxxxxxxxxxxxxxxx xxxxxxxxxxxxxxxxxxxxxxxx.
19 ¶	Paragraphing error	xxxxxxxxxxxxxxxxxxxxxxxx xxxxx. ↰ ¶ xxxxxxxxxxxxxxxxxxxxxxxx xxxxxxxxxxxxxxxxxxx.	xxxxxxxxxxxxxxxxxxxxxxxx xxxxx. xxxxxxxxxxxxxxxxxxxxx xxxxxxxxxxxxxxxxxxxxxxxx xxxxxxxxx.
20 *RO*	Run-on sentence	*RO* Beverly used to teach in Mexico it was great.	Beverly used to teach in Mexico. It was great.
21 *frag*	Fragment error	*frag* After they taught French in high school.	After finishing university, they taught French in high school.
22 *CS*	Comma splice	*CS* Carol has a house in Mexico, she loves it.	Carol has a house in Mexico. She loves it.

Symbols for parts of speech

Symbol	Explanation	Sentence marked with symbols	Corrected sentence
1 *v*	Verb	*v* Carol back from school at 5 p.m.	Carol comes back from school at 5 p.m.
2 *aux*	Auxiliary verb	*aux* When Beverly live in New York City?	When did Beverly live in New York City?
3 *pro*	Pronoun	*pro* Beverly loves family very much.	Beverly loves her family very much.
4 *prep*	Preposition	*prep* In 2003, Carol went Mexico.	In 2003, Carol went to Mexico.
5 *art.*	Article	*art.* Carol wants to visit friend in Japan.	Carol wants to visit a friend in Japan.
6 *adj*	Adjective	*wf* *use adj* This is a wonderfully book.	This is a wonderful book.
7 *adv*	Adverb	*wf* *use adv* They didn't write it quick.	They didn't write it quickly.
8 *conj*	Conjunction	*conj* Both of them like Chinese, Japanese, Thai food.	Both of them like Chinese, Japanese, and Thai food.